PERELMAN'S NEW RHETORIC
AS PHILOSOPHY AND METHODOLOGY
FOR THE NEXT CENTURY

Library of Rhetorics

VOLUME 1

SCOPE

The bookseries *Library of Rhetorics* is meant as a companion series to the international journal *Argumentation*. The bookseries and the journal should reinforce each other. The bookseries would mainly focus on:
- Argumentation *stricto sensu* (the theory of reasoning)
- Literary and legal rhetoric
- Rhetoric and the humanities
- Sociology and historical aspects of rhetorical thought
- Particular problems in rhetoric and argumentation.

PERELMAN'S NEW RHETORIC AS PHILOSOPHY AND METHODOLOGY FOR THE NEXT CENTURY

MIECZYSLAW MANELI

City University of New York, U.S.A.

Kluwer Academic Publishers

Dordrecht / Boston / London

Library of Congress Cataloging-in-Publication Data

```
Maneli, Mieczysław.
    Perelman's new rhetoric as philosophy and methodology for the next
century / by Mieczysław Maneli.
        p.   cm. -- (Library of rhetorics ; v. 1)
    Includes index.
    ISBN 0-7923-2166-9 (alk. paper)
    1. Perelman, Chaïm.  2. Rhetoric--Philosophy.  3. Philosophy,
Modern--20th century.  4. Methodology.  5. Reasoning.   I. Title.
II. Series.
    B4165.P474M36   1993
    160--dc20
                                                        93-18161
```

ISBN 0-7923-2166-9

Published by Kluwer Academic Publishers,
P.O. Box 17, 3300 AA Dordrecht, The Netherlands.

Kluwer Academic Publishers incorporates the publishing programmes of
D. Reidel, Martinus Nijhoff, Dr W. Junk and MTP Press.

Sold and distributed in the U.S.A. and Canada
by Kluwer Academic Publishers,
101 Philip Drive, Norwell, MA 02061, U.S.A.

In all other countries, sold and distributed
by Kluwer Academic Publishers Group,
P.O. Box 322, 3300 AH Dordrecht, The Netherlands.

Printed on acid-free paper

Printed in the Netherlands

Table of Contents

Author's Preface and Acknowledgments

This book was inspired by Chaim Perelman from my point of view. It is a monograph about his philosophy and methodology, but to a great extent it was personally initiated by him.

About two years ago before his premature death, Professor Perelman suggested in our very private conversation that I should write a concise handbook on New Rhetoric for the use of general public and university students. He assured me that he would do anything possible to help me to elaborate a "guide" to his own theory of argumentation. He stressed that he himself, for many reasons, did not want to undertake a task of being his own popularizer, promoter and a "chief de propaganda fide" (his own expression). In this period I was already an author of half a dozen essays and papers about New Rhetoric. During many international and national conferences I was adhering to the New Theory of Argumentation and have become known in various scholarly circles in Europe and America, as one of the proponents who was actively elaborating the new rhetorical premises.

In my own publications, I have been approaching step by step Perelman's theory and finally I embraced it as my own philosophy and methodology. My latest monographs, especially "Juridical Positivism and Human Rights" and "Freedom and Tolerance" were influenced by New Rhetoric's *Weltan-Schauung*.

We started to discuss the primer of the New Rhetoric and we felt very optimistic about the first specific outline. Unfortunately, his death interrupted our endeavor, but not for a long time. The wife of Professor Perelman, an unusually gifted and energetic scholar in her own right, Dr. Fela Perelman, was so greatly dedicated to his memory and to the Western heritage, that she tried to continue his work from where he left it unfinished. It was she and her daughter, Dr. Noemi Perelman-Mattis, who morally assisted me and they created such an atmosphere, that I was able to overcome various obstacles and to continue my research to present Perelman's opus magnum in a systematic and updated form.

Thanks to Dr. Guy Haarscher, I had a chance to spend some time in Brussels and to lecture at the Free University. In this way I became acquainted with the milieu and creative atmosphere in which Perelman was working.

Both Perelman's collaborators, Professors Haarscher and Ingber, shared with me their deep personal insights about origins, birth and phases of the development of the New Rhetoric. Without their good will, advice and creative comments, my personal knowledge would have been narrower.

I am grateful to the Chaim Perelman Foundation for their grant which enabled me to cover my expenses of collecting materials, editing and preparing the manuscript. Professor Michel Meyer was very instrumental in the negotiations with the publisher.

Mr. Raphael Lipski, treasurer of the Perelman Foundation, spent many hours with me, and shared his remembrances of Perelman's personality, his social and political activity.

I owe special thanks to Dr. Richard Kramer, whose friendship I cherish for a quarter of a century. He read and edited not only the entire text of the book, but he offered many critical remarks and constructive suggestions which helped me to revise my own ideas and to formulate them more clearly and precisely.

The first critical reader and editor was as usual Mrs. Elizabeth Previti. Professor Elzbieta Ettinger-Chodakowska, MIT, read this entire manuscript and shared with me her impressions. I owe special gratitude to my dear friend, Mrs. Stephanie Silvers for her steady help and moral support.

Needless to say, I am solely responsible for all the deficiencies of this book.

Mieczyslaw Maneli

Other publications by same author

Freedom and Tolerance (1984, 1987)
Juridical Positivism and Human Rights (1981)
War of the Vanquished (1971)
History of Political and Juridical Ideas, 5 vols, (1963–1968)
Foundations of Political Science, 3 vols, (1967–1968)
Machiavelli: A Monograph (1968)
Art of Politics (1967)
The Functions of the State (1963)
The Activity of a Socialist State (1957)

Preface

Chaïm Perelman's work is known all over the world. He was a professor at the Free University of Brussels and developed a theory of argumentation and a conception of justice which are among the major contributions to contemporary thought.

His theory of argumentation is extremely important because it addresses a fundamental philosophical and moral problem: the use of reason in action. Men act, choose ways and values. But the question is: how are they to make these aims compatible?

If it were possible to demonstrate once and for all, as traditional rationalist metaphysics wanted to do, that an orientation is the "true" one, the other possibilities would be reduced to error or absurdity. It would amount, for the "dissidents", to deny the validity of an objective demonstration. So their opinion would have no importance at all. Such a "demonstrative" conception of reason in action would thus negate tolerance and respect for the ideas of the others: we would only be confronted by true (demonstrated) and false statements concerning justice and the good life.

Now, as Perelman repeatedly said: "One does not argue about truth and falsehood". He was aware that moral and social life is too complex and subtle to be reduced to such an abstract opposition. He struggled during his whole life against the potential danger of intolerance coming from people who think they possess the truth in matters of ethics and politics.

But another danger, quite symmetrical to the first one, was also emphasized by Perelman: if demonstrative reason is inapplicable in human matters, will one conclude – as the positivists do – that moral choices are only subjective and reason is impotent inasmuch as ends and values are concerned? But then, Perelman argued, practical life would definitely be identified to the realm of violence and brute force.

Perelman had the merit of proposing a solution to this problem by refusing the two extreme terms of the alternative: in practical life, we can and must always give "good reasons", allowing us to persuade the others (and first to persuade ourselves) that a choice is preferable to another. But these good reasons have never the force and the constraining character of a demonstration: they are more fragile, less absolute, more "modest". And so we are never absolutely sure of the validity of our choices, which means that we can *learn* by dialoguing with the others.

Perelman drew such a conception of a weaker rationality from a reinterpretation of Aristotle's rhetoric. We can understand in such a context why the revival of the ancient art of argumentation by Perelman has so important moral, political, methodological and philosophical consequences.

Here comes Professor Maneli.

Perelman died in 1984, without having been able to accomplish the philosophical synthesis he had wanted to do. Maneli's project is to draw himself the philosophical consequences of the theory of argumentation. He is the author – among many important books – of *Freedom and Tolerance*, a master study he published more than a decade ago and which was highly regarded by Perelman.

In *Freedom and Tolerance*, Maneli already used Perelman's theory of argumentation to try to give a philosophical foundation to a pluralist, democratic and tolerant conception of society.

It was therefore quite natural that the Chaïm Perelman Foundation would ask Professor Maneli to write a book on New Rhetoric and its general significance in various domains.

Maneli knew Perelman personally, which allows him to link his life and work in a very subtle way (see the first chapter on "Perelman's spiritual personality"). In particular, Maneli discusses the origins and foundations of the New Rhetoric, its relation to dialectics, the political and moral problems related to it, the very important jurisprudential elements of the theory, and above all its humanist character. The final chapter of the book is dedicated to an attempt, revealing the great originality of Maneli's project, to systematize New Rhetoric as a philosophy and methodology for the Twenty-First Century.

Maneli tries to show that Perelman's theory of argumentation is what we need today if we want to cope with the difficulties of the post-communist world: beyond the rationalist dogmatism of Hegelian-Marxian dialectical rationality on the one hand, and the skeptical relativism of "post-modern" culture on the other hand, there is a place for a conception of the reasonable as defined above. Such a pluralist view of reason is related to a conception of justice which Perelman linked to his Jewish intellectual and existential background. All these problems are addressed with a remarkable clarity by Maneli. I am quite sure that his book will give all the scholars who work in one way or another on New Rhetoric the systematic perspective they lack and the philosophical instruments they need.

Guy Haarscher
Secretary General of the
Chaim Perelman Foundation

CHAPTER I

Introduction: New Thinking

1. PERELMAN'S SPIRITUAL PERSONALITY

This essay on the philosophy and methodology of Chaim Perelman is written by an author who enjoyed the friendship of and exchanged ideas, personally, with the founder of the New Rhetoric. I have been deeply influenced by his creative thinking and conclusions.

My recent scholarly publications have been written in the spirit of the New Theory of Argumentation. But in order to write in the spirit of that creative methodology one must also develop this methodology and philosophy according to the new circumstances and requirements of the subjects. I tried to do it during Perelman's life and his favorable opinions of my writings, especially his reviews of my two monographs, *Juridical Positivism and Human Rights* and *Freedom and Tolerance*, were the greatest encouragement for me.

It is a matter of fact that we live in a period when all kinds of ideologies in the east and in the west are collapsing. We have witnessed the bankruptcy of "Socialism" and also of liberalism and untamed capitalism. All the ideals of the last two centuries must be revised down to their foundations. The prognosis made by Chaim Perelman has been confirmed: there are no absolute truths in social and political ideologies. On the other hand, one should look for elements of truth, humanism progress, freedom, and tolerance in any political philosophy and socio-political system.

The New Rhetoric has become even more important and topical since the death of its Founder than it was during his lifetime when the divisions of the Cold War constituted a fertile soil for the uncritical acceptance of dogmas, ideas, and slogans.

The philosophy and methodology of Perelman is an instrument which can help to elaborate new ways of thinking and acting, new critical approaches to every social, political, and juridical institution, be they in the east or in the west. The traditional divisions of left and right, of progress and justice, of human rights and privacy, of state sovereignty and internal autonomy, must be revised extensively. Today the New Rhetoric, is the most consistent method of searching for new approaches.

1

Perelman's methodology and philosophy are important for all democratically minded people in our time. His contribution should be valued because
he was able to combine the universalistic with a very special attachment to
his own heritage. He acted predominantly in Belgium, yet at the same time
regarded it a *point d'honneur* to lecture in New York, Jerusalem, Warsaw,
and Paris.

Perelman's Polish education and excellent command of the Polish literary
language, his spiritual connection with the Polish humanistic liberal philosopher, Tadeusz Kotarbinski, and the Polish School of Logic were also significant.
They did not limit his horizons but added special elements to his general
outlook.

If one prefers to call Perelman a Polish Jew, then only in the sense
suggested by Czeslaw Milosz, the Nobel prize winner: special original category
of Jewish-European intellectual, different from all other Jewish and non-Jewish
categories of intellectualism.

Indeed he was a Belgian patriot always stressing his Belgian spiritual
association especially in the presence of foreigners. He consciously sought
to overcome all narrow nationalistic and caste barriers. He wanted to become
"menschlich" and *"all zu menschlich."* His striving for it was very typical
and amazingly western and cosmopolitan at the same time. He gained world
recognition going beyond his national frontiers.

Perelman's contribution to contemporary philosophy and the social sciences
must, as usual, be assessed in connection with western tradition and the
intellectual climate prevailing during the second half of our century.

Perelman, of course, did not simply revive Aristotle's ideas; he exceeded
them by far. Resurrecting old wisdom from oblivion and presenting it in light
of new conflicts and antagonisms, usually constitutes an innovation and a
significant step forward.

In this case one can state that Perelman tried to elaborate a methodology
and philosophy directed against a belief in "absolute truths" or "dogmas" which
constitute a *Weltanschauungsbasis*, not only of right- and left-wing dogmatic
ideologies, but also of any authoritarian – if not outright totalitarian –
tendencies even in modern, highly developed western, parliamentarian
democracies. He also opposed modern relativism in theories of politics, values,
law, and morality. He discarded various types of positivism or pragmatism
and especially the theory according to which value judgments must be made
arbitrarily in as much as they cannot withstand scientific inquiry; he regarded
these concepts as disastrous for scholarly thinking.

Nevertheless, he never questioned the historically progressive role of the
positivistic and pragmatic approaches; he only fought their limitations and
"deviation" from their initially productive way of thinking. But, once the
critical credo was transformed into unprincipled relativism, once formal logic
was used for dogmatic purposes, he raised his voice and announced that there
was a substantial difference between "rational" and "reasonable." Here his
departure from Descartes began. It reached its apogee in the following thesis:
Descartes is incorrect when he asserts that when two people express different

ideas concerning the same social situation, then at least one of them must be wrong. Perelman counters Descartes' assertion by saying that perhaps both are right, perhaps both views could be proven in the process of dialogue and argumentation, and finally, practically.

This concept has nothing to do with Tertulian's famous *credo quia absurdum*, but is based on the true dialectics of life: it is possible and reasonable to elaborate and realize different and contradictory social or political programs and one can establish that both are to a certain extent and for a certain time, beneficial for society.

Perelman believed that judgments not based on the categories of formal logic could still be reasonable, not irrational. Therefore, the category of reasonableness, as opposed to rationality based solely on formal logic, plays such an important role in his philosophy. I personally feel that this contribution opens new horizons and is an additional effective weapon in the fight against dogmatism.

This difference between Perelman's reasoning and that of his predecessors, especially the positivists and pragmatists, lies in an extensive notion of pluralism and dialogue. Dialogue, in his philosophy, not only becomes a simple exchange of ideas, but a social category which promotes an endless competition of arguments in order to establish the best possible solution in a given situation and at a given time. When however, even one of the factors of reality changes, even through a mere lapse of time, a valid cause arises to reopen dialogue and reassess the situation *ab initio*, from the very roots. During this reassessment nothing should be regarded as sacred or established once and for all.

Dialogue in the presence of an *unlimited* audience (another of Perelman's ideas) including scholars, authors, philosophers, politicians, and all who want to think, thus becomes a great criterion of relative truth and of relatively good solutions which nevertheless should, of course, be viewed as only temporary.

This approach is a creative rejection of all kinds of usurpation by formal logicians who allege that beyond the scope of formal reasoning any judgment can only be arbitrary and cannot be based on reason.

The ability to present one's own arguments is not in the philosophy of Perelman an eristical exercise only; indeed, it pertains to the essence of the search for truth and good solutions. I personally reached the same conclusion in my *Freedom and Tolerance* and presented it in the form of a rejection of the idea which had become so famous due, among others, to the fact that it found its way to the *Encyclopedia* of Diderot: there are many roads – it was written in the XVIIIth century–leading to error but *only* one path leads to truth; that is not so, I wrote in the spirit of Perelman's philosophy; there are *many* roads leading to truth as well.

This approach, which Perelman calls rhetorical or argumentative, enables us to elaborate a reasonable theory of the interpretation of law, with whose help we can overcome the dogmatic contradictions between "objectivists" and "subjectivists" in the theory of juridical interpretation. It is important in the legal profession to put aside the exaggerated roles of these theories. Perelman's philosophy enables us – as I tried to prove in my *Juridical Positivism and Human Rights* – to construct a reasonable and rationalistic theory of human rights and interpretation of law without referring to such ideas as "natural law," the "dictates of pure reason," not to mention the "divine right." The theory of Perelman also makes it possible to present reasonable arguments in favor of various social values based on the historical experience of mankind without leaving these reflections to the domain of arbitrary, predominantly *a priori* judgments of theologians, dogmatists and their like.

Perelman himself, when presenting his concept of justice and equity, gave a very good example how emotionally and politically charged theories of justice can become an object of fruitful scholarly analysis. Today one cannot even imagine a serious scholarly treatise on justice and equity without the subtle analyses provided by Perelman.

Professor Perelman died after his new Theory of Argumentation had already been established and had brought him well-deserved recognition. He had just entered the next phase of his creativity: elaborating and expanding the philosophical basis of his methodology. The new rhetoric was from its inception conceived as a new method of non-formal reasoning, a new type of western Rationalism – as it was already mentioned – which was for the first time consciously and consistently applied to the spheres of morality, values, jurisprudence and politics. When, however, in *The New Rhetoric* and in his subsequent writings, Perelman's methodology was substantiated and expanded, a new question inevitably arose what is the connection between the New Rhetoric as a method and metaphysics, understood in a very broad sense as a unity of ontology and epistemology? One could also ask this question in another way: is the New Rhetoric not a philosophy in itself? Does the further development of the rhetorical method not lead both to perfecting it as a method and as a general theory of being, values, social changes, and decision-making in politics? Perelman's closest friends, associates, and collaborators were discussing these problems with him for a long time. We were familiar with various concepts and nuances which his creative mind was conceiving, elaborating, and abandoning. Finally, he started to collect material and prepared himself mentally and philosophically to write his own course on metaphysics. The fact that he did not have a chance to finish this work, still doesn't undermine my conviction that the *New Rhetoric is a philosophy as well*.

The next higher stage in the development of the New Rhetoric was under way when death interrupted the author's endeavor. Those who are influenced by Perelman's thought continue to apply his ideas and develop them. This is the nature of Perelman's philosophy: to understand it is to apply it creatively.

All of us who knew Professor Chaim Perelman personally or were familiar with his work miss him immensely as a loyal, open friend and thinker, a fighter and a statesman. We all know that he had much more to say than he was able to express in his lifetime. But death, which interrupted his work, has been followed by strange consequences. Now, it is becoming more and more evident that his heritage is unfinished not because of this limitation but because of its greatness. His *magnum opus* is a harmonious construction of ideas which are both internally coherent and socially fruitful. His thoughts are well-shaped and form a fertile basis for building new philosophies of life, new ideals of freedom, tolerance, and progress. Today we see better than ever that Perelman's ideas will have an evergrowing impact on many spheres of philosophy, as well as juridical and political studies. This is a classic case of a great creator leaving the world after which his ideas become even more influential as their intellectual seeds proliferate and spread. I, who was privileged to share his personal attention and discussions, feel it my duty to popularize his ideas and to develop them. One owes this to his memory and to humanity.

Chaim Perelman was first of all a consistent rationalist, he believed in the power of human reason in the successful search for truth and for a reasonable organization of human relations. There were no taboos for him, no forbidden subjects. In his endeavors to promote the cause of reason and humanism, he had to overcome certain, sometimes sacred, axioms and rules. He found that denial, the Hegelian "Aufheben", was the only way to continue and to develop them. He continued to carry his banner of *raison* and *clarité*. He himself expressed his ideas "clearly and distinctly." He wrote in such a manner that everybody with a basic education, common sense, and willingness to know, could understand him. He was profound, but he wrote for ordinary people. He never flashily displayed his erudition; he spoke and wrote to persuade, to convince, and to impel others to think.

Of course, one can grasp the true benefits of this approach in analyzing specific problems. In *Faust* it was observed: "*grau, mein Freund, ist jede Theorie.*" Only the *Lebensbaum* (the tree of life) is eternally green and alone can be the supreme test of any theory. Perelman's theory is not "grau" (grey), but is an indispensable instrument to keep alive and green the tree of life.

2. SOCIAL ANTAGONISMS AND THE NEW RHETORIC

The New Rhetoric's many roots spread out among the social, political and intellectual fields. Perelman himself discussed only several sources of his inspiration. It was a clear, informative rendition.

He rejected the willingness to turn positivistic ethical questions and normative decisions over to arbitrariness and irrationalism. Another intellectual source for his new approach rested in consistent antidogmatic approach to the problem of truth. Even before his rhetorical period he stressed our need for a new way of thinking in order to overcome the contradictory and often dogmatic interpretation of relationships between relative truth and absolute truth and the endless mixup between objective and subjective aspects of the "objective truths."

He viewed with apprehension the excessive, if not arrogant, claims of formal, traditional, logic which appealed for acceptance as a general, universal tool for reasoning and for solving social problems. He never underestimated formal logic but he resisted applying it where it did not belong.

And lastly, after he began to regard pluralism as a way of life and a way of reasoning, he felt that a new concept of argumentation and persuasion had become necessary.

His sources were both – if one may call them such – positive and negative. He endeavored to check, while also to continue, various trends and elements.

We prefer to concentrate at the beginning on the social and methodological points of view of argumentation. Whatever terminology is used in this respect by Perelman himself and whatever his partial explanations may have been, there is no doubt that social contradictions, compounded by economic and ideological antagonisms were the first and foremost influences upon the thinking and feelings of the creator of the new theory of argumentation. Let be stressed that from the very beginning, this new theory of argumentation was meant to be an instrument for resolving social contradictions on a local, national, as well as international scale. It was also a method for healing the wounds caused by animosities arising from social and ideological struggles.

Especially during the last years of his life, Perelman was aware (and here I refer particularly to his famous and still underestimated interview with Dr. Wiktor Osiatynski in Bulgaria) that humanity had entered an exceedingly dangerous period. Class antagonisms were being deliberately, rather than spontaneously, extended to the sphere of international relations and proclaimed as the main cause of the Cold War. He knew that the Cold War had not simply been a struggle between the western and the eastern worlds, between socialism and capitalism – if one insists on using this terminology – but that it had an influence on all of humanity, every country and continent. Legitimate differences of opinions were easily and frequently elevated into political and ideological controversies, thereby precluding any possibility of reasonable resolution of the antagonisms. A simplistic interpretation of contradictions and animosities led to a unique sort of mental laziness and an anti-intellectual tendency to interpret all events as good or bad.

It was during this politically and ideologically precarious period, generally known as the Cold War that Perelman announced his studies on the New Rhetoric. His strong emphasis on dialogue as the indispensable and necessary instrument for achieving reasonable and peaceful solutions was augmented by his assertion that even in such tempestuous periods of world politics it was still possible to reach reasonable and peaceful understandings and solutions; it was a challenge to the world of his time with its high political ambitions and contradictory economic interests. Most important from the philosophical and psychological viewpoints is that Perelman challenged the prevailing intellectual stagnation. Today, more than ever, we recognize the heretofore underestimated aspect of his rhetorical challenge. Intellectual stagnation is also one of the most durable and vicious legacies of the Cold War divisions.

In his writings, but even more in his speeches, Perelman would stress the warning that we must think of all the consequences of a World War III which could terminate our civilization and all humanity too; something better than that must be found. Although he never stated it in so many words, it is a matter of fact that in the 1970's and 1980's he rejected the famous dictum of Karl von Clausewitz: "War is not merely a political act, but also a political instrument, a continuation of political relations, a carrying out of the same by other means." In our era, when the death of mankind is the foreseeable and the proximate logical outcome of a general nuclear war, the military extension of politics should be laid to rest forever. Therefore where recourse to military solutions is excluded the belligerent parties must be persuaded that they can reach an agreement, albeit an agreement everyone finds unattractive, on the basis of rhetorical dialogue.

Our chief emphasis should be that the inevitable contradictions in the modern world must be resolved in a peaceful manner. The highest virtue of any statesman or leader therefore must be his ability to enter into negotiations and live by the sword of persuasion instead of the sword of annihilation.

No wonder Perelman regarded his New Rhetoric as a method which could and should be used by people from any social or political system, that it could be used by despots and democrats alike, east and west. We know that sometimes this point has been taken out of context and severely criticized. It has even been said that a specialist in rhetorical argumentation could assume the role of an advisor not only to liberal democratic progressive forces, but also to despotic dogmatic reactionaries. That is not so, as we know. That was neither Perelman's intention nor his meaning. He merely believed that the principles of dialogue must be accepted by everyone in our time because the consequences of antagonism without dialogue cannot result in peace but only in a disastrous war with no desirable outcome possible.

Perelman was an ardent proponent of dialogue between Jews and Palestinians. As we know, he was prepared to participate in a dialogue even with representatives of the PLO. He had helped to arrange such a meeting, but the PLO representatives backed out at the last moment and he appeared alone at the conference room.

Of course he did not believe that official representatives of Israel or senior official of Jewish organizations should necessarily follow his example and seek such a dialogue at any time convenient to the terrorists of such an organization. Nevertheless, he believed that a philosopher and scholar should have special freedoms and privileges in order to be able to enter into difficult dialogues even with the devil himself without causing political consternation or uproar. On the other hand, however, he was certain that if intellectuals would meet and discuss the issues, sooner or later their influence would sway even the most hostile parties or governments.

As we see, Perelman's personal conduct exemplified another element of his philosophy. He believed that philosophers, and intellectuals generally, are obliged to be open-minded, tolerant, and prepared to enter into dialogues with everyone who reciprocates a desire for discussion. It would be needless, however, to speculate whether Perelman truly had the highest, unreserved esteem for fellow intellectuals. As was obvious, he criticized their attitudes, behavior, and the specific *trahison des clercs*.

Perelman believed nevertheless that the high regard accorded intellectuals in the modern world was occasioned by the existing social relations and the specific functions the intellectuals are required to perform these days. There must be an exchange of ideas among nations, countries, and people.

Participants must be able to engage in this exchange with neither political restraint nor any obligation to represent their own government. If dedicated intellectuals could accomplish this task efficiently, we would benefit. It they fail, everyone fails. Sooner or later, however, new intellectuals, more innovative and more socially prudent, emerge in all countries. In this respect Perelman agreed with C. Wright Mills, the famous American sociologist, who in the dark days of the 1960's, albeit himself persecuted by the scholarly establishment of Columbia University, proclaimed that there must be a direct dialogue between western and Soviet intellectuals because they were the only ones qualified to alter the calamitous course of events. The lack of such a dialogue C. Wright Mills regarded as one of the main *Causes of World War III*, one of the last books of his short life. What many regarded farcical and utopian in the sixties, and led them to treat Mills with polite contempt, became the unfolding way of life nearly twenty years later.

Once we entered this new situation in the mid-eighties, almost unimaginable in the days of C. Wright Mills and Perelman, it became more urgent to intensify our efforts to popularize the New Rhetoric and to continue the work of its founder. We must add new bricks to the structure of his wonderful edifice. The new world situation and the new circumstances in every single country and every political system, call for creative application of the New Theory of Argumentation.

Two additional elements should be given special consideration. The first is Perelman's concept of the "flow of argumentation." He himself rarely used that expression in his writings. That is not very important to us however. The New Rhetoric after all was conceived as a theory of the *process of argumentation* which can never be stopped although every phase in this endless process should have a clear ending in order to give the participants an opportunity for deeper reflection and to enable them to put into practical effect the results of the intellectual exchange achieved up to that point.

Argumentation for Perelman was an infinitely progressive process, one that consisted of various phases and stages. Argumentation is a process which is simultaneously practical and intellectual. This aspect of the New Rhetoric, as we know, has usually been undervalued by theorists and at times even disregarded by critics, both friendly and unfriendly.

The New Rhetoric should be regarded as a theory rooted in social and political practice; it assists reflection and it is intended at the same time to serve practical purposes, to solve problems as skillfully as possible in the most enlightened manner that is feasible at any given stage. In this way, Perelman tried to solve the famous and exaggerated contradiction between relative and absolute truth. We should accept the following construction, he advised us: every stage of our analysis, investigation, and reasoning leads to certain conclusions which can be regarded as a partial or relative truth. Such truth is a partial reflection of reality; it is a point, a stage in the understanding of the processes which take place in society. This reflection is incomplete and cannot be an absolutely correct presentation and understanding of events because, as Sir Francis Bacon observed in his *Novum Organum* – our minds are like uneven mirrors. On the other hand, however, this partial truth, always the result of serious investigation and analysis, is part and parcel of the endless process of searching for absolute truths, an achievement we strive for and will be able to attain as time goes on. Absolute truths in the future, according to the rhetorical view, will consist of the sum of endless partial truths.

In this way we are able to combat two kinds of dangers: absolute relativism and absolute dogmatism. We can always answer from the rhetorical point of view – and here rhetoric will coincide with the Greek, Hegelian, and Marxian dialectic – that absolute relativism is unreasonable, that it is a *contradictio in adjecto* because in every real intellectual achievement and in every kind of progressive, enlightened, practical activity are ingrained elements of truth. On the other hand, one can answer every dogmatist that elements of relativism are inevitable in every ideology, philosophy or theory. Modesty and tolerance are therefore necessary for every thinker and statesman, for every theorist and politician.

Our assertion that the New Rhetoric is the philosophy and methodology of the turn of the twentieth century is based not only on the merits of the New Theory of Argumentation, but also on an analysis of our actual and ideological state of affairs. The decline of ideologies throughout the world was already evident during the lifetime of C. Wright Mills, and even more so of Perelman. During recent years, however, this decline has terminated in total bankruptcy, not only of the Communist system but of its ideological underpinnings as well.

The Communist system was unable to solve basic economic and nationalistic problems although it provided some progress in many areas of life. According to Marx and Lenin, the superiority of the Communist system would be demonstrated only when the standard of living and the productivity of labor rise higher under the socialist regime than under the capitalist. During recent decades this basic test has demonstrated the superiority of the relatively free market system over governmental bureaucratic centralization. Today it seems that the Communist revolution was able to resolve many social, political and economic problems efficiently, yet only partially, especially in the fields of education and science in underdeveloped nations. When these nations had reached a higher stage of development after enormous effort, victimization, and exploitation by the government bureaucracy, it became obvious that the new revolutionary system not only had shot its bolt but had itself become a new "prison" bottling up the productive forces, if the famous expression of *The Communist Manifesto* is allowed.

The prophecy which Marx and Engels voiced with regard to capitalism became fully applicable to centralized, bureaucratic socialist society. The full impact of the bankruptcy of the socialist system, from the material and ideological viewpoints, is still unknown to us, but we may expect further accelerated changes all over the world. We are referring to the bankruptcy of both the Communist ideology and system, since they were the only pre-conceived utopia which certain nations endeavored to bring to life in modern times. The tragic results of this utopian endeavor confirm that humanity should at long last give up hope for any preconceived (necessarily utopian!) doctrines which would cure all human ills and disasters.

With the fall of the Communist systems nations are uncritically offered a new panacea to remedy the communist and socialist ills, the free market economy. We know from western experience that there are different forms of free market economy and no western pattern can be imposed mechanically upon any post-Communist society. We also know that the situation in western societies is far from ideal. There are many social and economic ills which the western democracies have been unable to resolve. It is therefore naive for eastern nations and western politicians to recommend the western economic systems and the idealized western parliamentary institutions as a new panacea, as an ideal which must and can be achieved.

What we see may be described as a transition from the Communist system to another, possibly more efficient, more democratic, more free way of life, not determined by any fixed norms or means. Every eastern and western experience must be examined from the very beginning, both the means and the goals. For this purpose the New Rhetoric is an ideal tool. It is a philosophy and a method for evaluating new visions, targets, and situations thoroughly. This philosophy and methodology does not guarantee that mistakes will be avoided or prevented, but it does give maximum certitude that the errors will be recognized and corrected. We do not know what the end of the road is, but we have to move in a manner that promises to be more efficient and less painful than previous methods have been.

It is not, however the bankruptcy of Communism as an ideology alone that is so important in our era. The transformation of the capitalist system is also inevitable. With the bankruptcy of Communism, the primitive slogans, touting anti-Communism, or the "evil empire," have also been compromised.

Experience in western countries on both sides of the Atlantic shows that our freedoms and democracy are constantly being endangered, that assaults on the western democratic system occur frequently. We know the extreme form of capitalist authoritarianism; fascism, nazism, clerico-religious fundamentalism, and McCarthyism in America. We also know that various totalitarian tendencies are in evidence in the west, including so called "creeping totalitarianism."*

There are strong tendencies in all western countries to restrict the power

---

* Mieczyslaw Maneli: *Freedom and Tolerance*, pp. 293–311.

of the parliament in favor of the executive. We are aware that there are various forms of militarism (usually combined with industrial and financial interests), and efforts to undermine freedom of information, the press, and our cherished concept of privacy. We observe the increasing power of big business and we know that at times governments are inefficient, if not helpless, in their efforts to restrict the powers of monopolies over the life of nations.

Let us reiterate: there are no ready recipes on how to rearrange the lives of western nations to make them more tranquil, secure and free. We do know that far reaching reforms are inevitable. The method of New Rhetoric is becoming more and more useful and irreplaceable to achieve these purposes.

Let us discuss several areas that connect the New Rhetoric with social and political problems.

The material sources for New Rhetorical thought, as already stressed, are social contradictions and antagonisms. We know that according to Communist and socialist theories and certain forms of liberal ideology, social Darwinism, and the theology of liberation, it is class struggle, traditionally ascribed to Marxism, that allegedly is one of the most important, decisive social issues which could determine all others. According to the New Rhetoric it would be unreasonable to deny the existence of class conflicts. The New Rhetoric, however, would never regard class antagonism as the only or the leading one under all circumstances. This over-simplification is perhaps not even Marxian, but it was typical for Lenin, Stalin, and their successors in the Soviet Union and in all so called Communist or Marxist Movements all over the world.

From the rhetorical point of view the class struggle may be viewed as one of the important conflicts of modern society, but by no means should it be considered the sole or even the decisive conflict. We know from experience that religious and national conflicts are at times more important, evoke more passion, more hatred, and more solidarity.

We also know that in the Communist countries themselves it was not a truly Marxian class conflict that existed between the majority of society and the new ruling group (or class – as Djilas wrote), it was a conflict between all society on the one hand and the state and party apparatus on the other, between the tendency toward freedom and democracy, and the opposing trend that supported the oppressive totalitarian institutions. Today, as the Communist regimes are collapsing, we note that the lines of the front are drawn unclearly and tend to zig-zag. There are members of the former ruling institutions and privileged administrations who actively endeavored to support democracy and renewal. There were *aparatchiks*, including Gorbachev, Yeltsin, and Shevardnaze, who raised their hands against the Party and bureaucracy. The results were disastrous for the Communist super elites in the East European communist states. Nevertheless, we have learned from the Polish, Czech, Hungarian, Bulgarian, and even Soviet and the East German examples that even those who ranked highest in hierarchy had betrayed their own system, their own totalitarian "superstructure," and voluntarily exited the historical arena without bloodshed. This phenomenon is meaningful.

These occurrences demonstrated that sometimes new ideas, developed in a process of mutual exchange and persuasion (in an actual dialogue at the round table conferences in Poland in 1988 and 1989), can undermine and eventually even prevail against an apparently invincible military, security, and administrative establishment.

These examples are important proof that the New Rhetoric's belief in the ability of dialogue to resolve the most acute and profound conflicts in certain circumstances is quite realistic. It represents true realism, as against ostensibly realistic postures and attitudes against, what C. Wright Mills called, "crackpot realism."

Let us also remember the specifics of McCarthy's terror in the United States. It seemed to many observers that his rise to power was invincible, that he could demoralize and terrorize the nation and no one dared stand against him. After some time, however, as we know, the star of Joseph McCarthy began to dim and darken as a result of a loss of Republican control of the Senate and McCarthy's loss of his committee chair. He lost his influence. He and his followers lost their overblown authority and powers forever. The public had shared the illusion that he was as unconquerable as Bertold Brecht's *Arturo Ui*. The public was wrong.

These are examples of how the power of reasoning and persuasion is able to overwhelm blind and naked terror, be it ideological or physical.

These events show that there is a close link between enlightened reason, politics, and morality. At certain times, under specific circumstances, the power of moral good and reason can become decisive in crushing despotic, reactionary, evil forces. The past years, which have not been attractive, have nevertheless produced many examples to illuminate the rhetorical concept that moral norms can be reasonable and justified, that it is possible to prove clearly that moral solutions are better and more useful to society than "crackpot realism," or the realism of *"Plattheiten"* (platitudes) baptized as *Wahrheiten* (truths).

Once more we have reached the same conclusions: since we know of no ultimate goal on the road we are traveling, we should at least strive for the best solutions we can find for existing problems. Without wasting time and effort on new impossible dreams we should bend our efforts to attain relative truth, partial solutions, and attempt to gain something reasonable and therefore possible and attainable. According to the principles of the New Rhetoric we must analyze our situation from top to bottom. Then we should either continue doing what we were doing or discard even widely held premises whose time has passed.

We should not be afraid that someone will say that we are mistaken or inconsistent because we have changed our methods or our goals. According to Rhetorical thinking, there is no virtue in being stubborn or in defending a wrong course, or in continuing a policy which experience has discredited and serves no real interests. We should not pursue anything for the sake of "firmness," or "coherence," or "holding together," or for the sake of "principles."

The New Rhetoric is the only philosophy which extols those who hesitate, reflect, and then change their course of action. According to rhetorical political philosophy, the only true moral and social virtue is our ability to reconsider, to reenter into dialogue, to keep an open mind, to be flexible, open to suggestions, and willing to follow new, reasonable advice. This rhetorical approach counters the traditional almost biblical admonition to go straight ahead, deviating neither to the right nor to the left. The New Rhetoric may be the only philosophy that praises those who ruminate, hesitate, are reluctant, doubtful, but ultimately able to act prudently.

We, in the western democracies have survived periods of increasing and decreasing state intervention; we have lived through various phases of the welfare state; in the U.S. under various forms of the New Deal, the Fair Deal, the New Frontier, the Great Society, and "supply economics." With them we have observed a revival of certain forms of old conservatism connected with such names as Ronald Reagan and Margaret Thatcher. Now we observe new turns in the life of every western and particularly every European country, and in the life of all of Europe itself. Once more we observe that every dogmatic idea and "ism" has either been rejected, or, as we feel today, should have been rejected. New roads, new methods, new goals, must be found. We have no ideology today which could serve as a signpost, a *Wegweiser*. Once more rhetorical thinking must be called upon to explore and to probe the unknown.

Following the evident bankruptcy of traditional liberalism and neo-liberalism, traditional conservatism and neo-conservatism, traditional pacifism and neo-militarism, traditional imperialism and neo-colonialism, of various forms of socialism and communism, we find ourselves on barren ground, devoid of any acceptable, political theory or ideology able to mobilize the imagination and vital forces of societies. We must begin in a very modest way, yet at the same time, we must discuss new ideas hopefully in an endless process of rhetorical dialogue.

These are the reasons why we believe that the New Rhetoric is the only philosophy and methodology which remains standing on the battlefield at the end of our century. This philosophy and methodology does not promise any miraculous solutions or any new roads to paradise. At any rate, we reject the notion of an earthly paradise as preposterous, unproductive, and sterile.

Perelman laid the foundations for the New Rhetoric as a new philosophy and methodology, but he was unable to complete his labors. Indeed, according to his own theory, this work can never be brought to completion; events always outdistance thought. We should try to develop our Rhetorical philosophy and methodology as an instrument that serves the people in their perennial struggle for freedom and justice.

The various sources of the New Rhetoric which we mentioned at the beginning of this chapter and in other parts of this book are a matter of particular importance. We stressed that the creator of New Rhetoric found his intellectual inspiration in positive and negative roots. Why?

Perelman needed to promote his new way of thinking in the midst, at times, of bitter controversies on many fronts and against various concepts. He rejected several of them outright. Others he tried to assimilate, at least in part. The necessity for campaigns against critics and the defense and elaboration of his own novel ideas resulted in situations which nearly every author of new theories must encounter. After the publication of his initial writings Perelman had to explicate certain aspects of his theory more comprehensively. Such a necessity led to exaggeration or distortions at times either in the wholeness of the image of this theory or of some particular element of his methodology.

Since Perelman is no longer with us to clarify and answer all questions, we present this theory, not as a concise repetition of its founder's writings, but as a presentation of the inner logic of the system. Not only will his wishes and intentions be followed, they will be presented in a truly balanced and complete way. To this task we will apply the famous maxims used by the interpreters of the first codes of civil law at the turn of our century: *par la code civile mais au de la code civile*, meaning, with the principles of the New Rhetoric to reach beyond the present corpus of rhetorical writings.

This suggestion has nothing to do with revisionism; we intend neither to revise nor change the basic principles of rhetorical theory or methodology. But we do find ourselves in a completely new situation from his. We are relieved for the stresses and immediate pressures of constant attacks or criticism arising from the novelty of the New Rhetoric, a luxury denied the master himself. In the comfort of ample time we can present a balanced, well-rounded view of all elements of the New Theory of Argumentation taken together.

It was Perlman's custom to preface some of his works with the analytical aspects of the New Rhetoric and stress the necessity for an unprejudiced approach to rhetorical dialogue, one devoid of preconceived judgments, entrenched beliefs or dogmas. Although the beginnings of serious discussions should be free of fixed judgments, if possible, the aim should be to extract not only facts but general conclusions during the exchange of ideas.

The purpose of dialogue is to separate the meaningful from the trivial, to weigh facts and judgments, not in order to assign equal weight to them, but instead to differentiate their values and thereby order the formless mosaic into a reasonable functional entity which can be used for practical purposes and for further theoretical investigation.

The purpose of rhetorical analysis is to avoid a sterile accumulation of facts, it aims to construct a reasonable, purposeful, reordering and re-evaluation of data. Rhetorical analysis and synthesis should not serve to reinforce skepticism in itself and for itself – to use a Kantian expression – but it should be treated as an instrument of skepticism seeking to overthrow the old gods in order to develop a new set of ideas, a new rational pattern of acting and searching.

The New Rhetoric does not mourn the present general bankruptcy of ideologies, exclaiming *"De profundis"* or *"Kadish"*, but it does try to establish what was productive in the rejected systems, what was unproductive, what was reasonable or unreasonable, what was workable and fruitful or damaging and unmanageable. We find ourselves today in a great historical cemetery of ideas and systems of politics and economics.

Nevertheless, our task is not to despair but to search for values. Values that can be reassessed, reused, recycled, and reassembled into a new set of projects, laws, and institutions. This is the gist of the New Rhetoric, it is ideological and non-ideological at the same time. Our Theory of Argumentation therefore can be applied as a supra-political, non-partisan method of synthesis.

CHAPTER II

The Origins and Foundations of the New Rhetoric

1. THE INITIAL DILEMMA: REASON AND MORALITY

In the essay, "The New Rhetoric: A Theory of Practical Reasoning," Perelman tells of his own intellectual evolution. In his first study on justice, published in 1945, we already find elements of doubt in the concept that an insurmountable barrier exists between the judgment of facts, and values.

He was deeply dissatisfied with a philosophical inquiry carried on within the limits of logical empiricism because it "was not able to provide an ideal of practical reason, that is, the establishment of rules and models for reasonable action."[1]

In this frame of mind he asked himself: " . . . is there a logic of value judgments that makes it possible for us to reason about values instead of making them depend solely on irrational choices, based on interest, passion, prejudice, and myth?"[2]

Perelman was not prepared to accept any from of subjectivism, skepticism, absolutism, or intuitionalism in his theory of value; he could not accept existentialist subjectivism either, although he appreciated the existentialist criticism of positivist empiricism and rationalistic idealism.

A clue pointing at a solution of his dilemma was given Perelman by the method employed by the German logician Gottlob Frege who analyzed the reasoning used by mathematicians. The result of these investigations and the tracing of the actual, empirical and logical reasoning to achieve value judgments by moralists, politicians, and authors are documented in *The New Rhetoric*.

Perelman writes:

For almost ten years Mme. L. Olbrechts-Tyteca and I conducted such an inquiry and analysis. We obtained results that neither of us has ever

---

[1] Chaim Perelman, A Theory of Practical Reasoning in: The Great Ideas of Today, 1970, *Encyclopedia Britannica*, Chicago, 1970, p. 280.
[2] *Ibid.*

expected. Without either knowing or wishing it, we had rediscovered a part of Aristotelian logic that had been long forgotten or, at any rate, ignored and despised. It was the part dealing with dialectical reasoning, as distinguished from demonstrative reasoning. . . . We called this new, or revived, branch of study, devoted to analysis of informal reasoning, *The New Rhetoric*.[3]

In this way the classic rhetoric was revived. But a renaissance is never simply a rebirth of the past. It has new elements and operates in a new manner under the new circumstances.

The New Rhetoric was born as a result of the practical and theoretical needs posed by the social and intellectual development of our century. Traditional empiricism, positivism, neopositivism, pragmatism, rationalism, and all their new forms were unable to answer the pressing topical questions of our day. The new requirements of life were urgent; people had to make decisions, they wanted to make them in a reasonable way. Especially in the twentieth century, we have seen successive waves of irrationalism by right and left wing totalitarianisms, not only in the emerging nations, but also in all well-established western democracies.[4] From the very beginning, *The New Rhetoric* has served as a method to analyze aspects of life which go beyond the purview of formal logic, thereby being relegated to methods usually far from the conscious application of reason.

2. RATIONAL AND REASONABLE: MONISM AND PLURALISM

The New Rhetoric has three basic elements which constitute its methodological basis as a philosophy of consistent rationalism:
– a new solution for the relationship between the reasonable and the rational;
– the problem of the audience;
– the problem of the dialogue.

There have always been intellectuals who believed that when one presents a clear argument, truthfully and logically substantiated, the mere power of the syllogism and truth should be sufficient to make a definitive impact on the minds of everyone able to think.

Such intellectuals adhere to Descartes who said that if two men have contrary judgments about the same thing, one at least must be mistaken and irrational, although it may be that both are in error. At any rate, as Descartes wrote, if the reasoning of either were certain and evident, he would be able to convince his opponent of its truth.[5]

---

[3]   *Ibid.*, p. 281.

[4]   Cf. Stephen Haseler in *Commentary*, vol. 64, No 2, August, 1977, p. 80. Let us remember that already in 1939 George Orwell observed that a simple restatement of the obvious had become a duty for the intelligent man. The situation has not improved in the last half century.

[5]   Perelman analyzes this idea in, "Disagreement and Reasonableness of Decisions," p. 2.

The point of departure of the theory of argumentation is different: according to the New Rhetoric, the Cartesian claims are excessive and unreasonable. It is Perelman's contention that both parties may have good, reasonable opinions because human, practical, political, and moral problems cannot be reduced to the antinomy, true or false. There are problems which cannot even be presented in the categories of formal logic, they cannot be syllogistically expressed or proven. Diverse opinions can be *reasonable* at the same time because there is a difference between what is rational and what is reasonable. This distinction lies at the heart of Perelman's New Rhetoric and Pluralism.[6]

According to various forms of philosophical and juridical positivism, formal logic is the sole tool of demonstration and verification. If what is rational is so narrowly defined, nearly the entire sphere which is concerned with action, including politics and morality, "is turned over to the irrational."[7]

This is the case with the popular and influential utilitarian approach.

The only reasonable decision would seem to be one that is in conformity with the utilitarian calculations. If so, all ends would be reduced to a single one of pleasure or utility, and all conflicts of values would be dismissed as based on futile ideologies.[8]

The reduction of the rational to a single principle leads to either *irrational pluralism*, or to *monism*. Monism of values is usually both irrational and unreasonable. Monism often has been used by authoritarian regimes, especially those pretending to have a rational basis ("crackpot realism" – see below).

The official Soviet Stalinist theory of morality, for instance, has introduced the following generally known axiom as the basis of socialist ethics: anything which helps to achieve the victory of communism all over the world is moral.[9] This concept obviously reduces the problems of morality to the requirements of current political tactics, although one could easily "prove" that once the given premises are accepted, all the conclusions concerning morality, being syllogistically correct, are rational. But, are they reasonable? Are they humane?

The same manner of reasoning could be applied to the logically correct conclusions which the Nazis drew from their premises, namely that the good of the *pure* German race should be regarded as the highest criterion of politics, law, and morality. How can these "rational" Nazi conclusions be refuted? Are logical, positivistic methods sufficient? The Nazi, Stalinist, and other inhumane ideologies can only be proved unreasonable by expanding the concept of reason beyond formal logic.

[6] The problem of pluralism will be discussed later.

[7] Chaim Perelman, *A Theory of Practical Reasoning*, p. 54.

[8] *Ibid.*, p. 55.

[9] P. Kolonitsky, "Communist Morality and Religious Morality," *Molodoy Bolshevik*, Nov. 1951, "Communist morality serves the cause of the construction of communism . . . " p. 53, "The whole ideology of communism, including communist morality, is subordinated to the cause of the liberation of the toilers." p. 60.

. . . if one is not prepared to accept such a limitation to a monism of values in the world of action and would reject such a reduction on the ground that the irreducibility of many values is the basis of our freedom and of our spiritual life; if one considers how justification takes place in the most varied spheres – in politics, morals, law, the social sciences, and, above all, in philosophy – it seems obvious that our intellectual tools cannot all be reduced to formal logic . . .[10]

The New Rhetoric does not eliminate formal logic and does not reject the value of syllogisms concerning deduction and induction, but reserves a proper place for them in the totality of human reasoning. The concept of reasonable is inherently pluralistic; it is incompatible with all pretensions of monism or totalitarianism.

The distinction between the "rational" and the "reasonable" is not new. It has been discussed almost since the rise of modern rationalism, although under various names and terminologies.

Both words, rational and reasonable, derive from the same substantive; both connote a conformity to reason, but they are rarely interchangeable; one would call a deduction which conforms to the rules of logic rational, but not necessarily reasonable. A compromise however, may be called reasonable. Let no one forget: a rational decision may be unreasonable, and vice versa.

For example: Perelman analyzes Godwin's famous argument that there is no rationality in loving one's own father more than other persons unless it is possible to prove that one's father is a better human being than other men. Perelman comments that Godwin's thinking may be logical and rational, but who would call it reasonable, or humane?

This example and many others like it indicate that "the idea of reason is shown in at least two diametrically opposed ways."[11]

This observation is one of the most important philosophical premises constituting the foundation of political, juridical, and moral pluralism: narrowly interpreted rationalism may lead to monism and absolutism; reasonableness, to a pluralistic vision of the world.

The *rational* may be described as what "corresponds to mathematical reason; for some it is a reflection of divine reason, which grasps necessary relations."[12] The *rational* imposes its outlook on all reasoning beings because "it owes nothing to experience, or to dialogue, and depends neither on education, nor on the culture of a milieu or an epoch." It is "associated with self-evident truths."[13]

According to Bertrand Russell "the rational man would only be an inhuman monster."[14]

---

[10] Chaim Perelman, *A Theory of Practical Reasoning*, p. 55.
[11] Chaim Perelman, *The Rational and the Reasonable*.
[12] *Ibid.*
[13] *Ibid.*

The man who tries to be consistently rational separates reason from his other faculties. He is a one-sided being, functioning like a machine.

The reasonable man, on the other hand, is not always "rational." He is influenced by "common sense," or, "good sense," and endeavors to do what is accepted by his own milieu, and if possible, by all. He takes into account changing circumstances, social evolution, sensitivity, the development of morality, the changing criteria of decency. For, "the reasonable of today is not the reasonable of yesterday . . . "[15] Without such a broad concept of the reasonable, reason would be converted into a conservative fortress, into an instrument of ossification, rather than a means by which the obsolete is repudiated. What is reasonable changes as mankind changes. A reasonable individual at any time can live within a variety of groups, with many ideals and philosophies. He is prepared to live in a pluralistic world.

What is rational can easily lead to biased, socially inadmissible conclusions; when this happens, Perelman writes, we must re-evaluate the whole system. In law, he continues, the idea of "the reasonable corresponds to an equitable solution."[16]

In general, "reasonable" opposes the uncritical acceptance of established reality; it promotes pluralistic change; the rational pertains to stability.

There is an amazing similarity between Perelman's concept of the *rational* and C. Wright Mills' idea of "crackpot realism." Mills uses this expression in many books and essays referring to the Eastern and Western rulers and their pseudo-intellectualism. Mills wrote:

> In the American white-collar hierarchies and in the middle levels of the Soviet "intelligentsia" – in quite differing ways but with often frightening convergence – there is coming about the rise of the crackpot realist. All these types embody a common ethos: rationality without reason.[17]

Mills accuses both world ruling groups of rationalizing the rules of the game leading to world-catastrophies. To cope with their "unreason" they appeal to logic and to realism. According to them, to be a "utopian" means merely to acknowledge values other than those accepted by the power-elites.

> But in truth, are not those who in the name of realism act like crackpots, are they not the utopians? Are we not now in a situation in which the only practical realistic down-to-earth thinking and acting is just what these crackpot realists call 'utopian?'[18]

Here we approach yet another meaning of "unreasonableness": it defends

---

[14]   *Ibid.*

[15]   *Ibid.*

[16]   There is, incidentally, also a link between the dialectic of the reasonable and the dialectic of justice and equity.

[17]   C. Wright Mills, *Power, Politics & People*, ed. Irving Louis Horowitz (New York: Oxford University Press, 1974), p. 393.

[18]   *Ibid.*, p. 402.

what is possible and desirable; it does not capitulate to "necessary reality." Rationalists accept reality as "given", as a premise, as something "necessary," whereas the truly reasonable man tries to overcome what has become obsolete or otherwise undesirable.

Limited realism, or rather pseudo-rationalism, serves today as the philosophical foundation of modern, "mindless" conservatism.[19]

> While the intellectuals have been embraced by the new conservative gentility, the silent conservatives have assumed political power . . . these men have replaced mind by the platitude . . . so widely accepted that no counter-balance of mind prevails against them. Such men as these are crackpot realists, who, in the name of realism have constructed a paranoid reality . . .[20]

Mills argues that various sociological and political concepts are a modern "rationality" without reason; we prefer to call it "rationalism without reasonableness." They justify the social status quo and conservative mindlessness, a priori inimical to any innovation, to democratic pluralism. Modern rationalism may tend toward uniformity, toward *Gleichschaltung*, whereas the reasonable always opposes uniformity, undermines any form of absolute order, and promotes pluralism in every sphere of life, in the material and spiritual, the economic and the political.

As applied to morality and politics, the New Rhetoric represents the view that one can and should find a reasonable basis for justifying the norms of behavior as well as of political norms.[21]

Many philosophers since Hume have argued that it is impossible to demonstrate that one set of moral rules is preferable to another.

The New Rhetoric asserts that if logicians dismiss the mere possibility of preferences based on reason in the sphere of the "ought" (Sollen) then we must enlarge the domain of the logicians' investigations. The enlargement would complement formal logic "through the study of what since Socrates has been called *dialectics* . . . I prefer to qualify it as argumentation, and contrast it with formal logic conceived as the theory of demonstrative proof."[22]

One should never overlook the fact that after all moral principles are formulated because there are reasons for formulating them. Therefore one should argue whether they should have been adopted at all, and if so, how they should be applied to given situations and controversies.

Positivists assimilate the justification of norms into the logical demon-

---

[19] There are conservatisms which officially are based on irrationalistic ideas, but the modern western and eastern conservatisms present themselves as rather rationalistic social orders or movements.

[20] C. Wright Mills, *op. cit.*, pp. 603–610. Mills refers the same characteristics to the communist and capitalist "realists" and rationalists.

[21] Chaim Perelman, *The Justification of Norms*, p. 1 Leonard G. Miller, Koral Scepticism, Philosophy and Phenomenological Research, 1961, vol. XII, pp. 239–245.

[22] *Ibid.*, p. 4.

stration of propositions. The question of truth in our behavior (its principles) is meaningless, because our actions and decisions cannot be "true." They can be described as correct, expedient, reasonable, equitable, thoughtful, conforming to moral norms, or legal provisions. Our decisions and actions are of course based on information concerning facts. The information may be true or false, and truthfulness or falsity may influence our decisions and behavior.[23]

The New Rhetoric is not a theory for pure contemplation; it is a theory of argumentation for practical purposes in order to find a way to make the most reasonable, efficient, and just decisions which might gain the maximum support of a public divided by various controversies. It is a theory which consciously helps to make practical but reasonable decisions, directly aiming at action.

3. DIALOGUE AND AUDIENCE

Dialogue is the form and the soul of the process of argumentation. From the rhetorical viewpoint, discourses in the courts are a form of dialogue which is also one of the philosophical bases of American and European juridical theory and practice.

The first precondition for the existence of dialogue is an interest of at least two participants in an exchange of ideas and in gaining the adherence of intellects.

A second precondition for the existence of dialogue is freedom for the participants. The interlocutor should not be afraid to raise questions and use counterarguments. One cannot gain the adherences of those who fear or hesitate to participate actively in the dialogue.

Every speaker or writer knows his *audience* more or less and knows the public he wants to address.

"We consider it preferable to define an audience, for the purposes of rhetoric, as the ensemble of those whom the speaker wishes to influence by his argumentation."[23]

The concept of the audience is very important in the structure of the New Rhetoric.

At times one tries to persuade one individual, at other times, whole social groups. A speaker should know what distinguishes one social environment from the other. He should know "the social functions exercised by its listeners."[24] The speaker or writer should always be aware that his audience is changing all the time, therefore the truly great orator must know the art of "continuous adaptation."[25] But Perelman, like Demosthenes, does not

---

[23] Chaim Perelman. "The New Rhetoric," *op. cit.*, p. 19.
[24] *Ibid.*, p. 21.
[25] *Ibid.*, p. 23.

identify "adaptation" with a reduction of rhetoric to the level of mere "flattery." The New Rhetoric is not the art of hypocrisy:

> . . . it must not be overlooked that the orator is nearly always at liberty to give up persuading an audience when he cannot persuade it effectively except by the use of methods that are repugnant to him. It should not be thought, where argument is concerned, that it is always honorable to succeed in persuasion, or even to have such an intention.[26]

We have approached what the New Rhetoric is not. It is not the art of using immoral means for immoral ends. It is not the art of employing questionable methods to achieve a goal. The Rhetorical argumentation can be used by despotic, or totalitarian rulers. The New Rhetoric, however, presupposes a free dialogue with a public free of fear which cannot occur under despotism. Such a dialogue is required because only an active audience will sooner or later be able to detect deliberate lies and misrepresentations, thereby correcting error.

When argumentation fails to achieve its desired effect, that still does not mean its premises were completely wrong, unjust, or unfounded. Arguments can be rejected by an audience for various reasons, but lies in a free exchange of arguments can be brought to light sooner that under many other circumstances.

The New Rhetoric does not take anything for granted. And Perelman's struggle against all the open and hidden vestiges of the theory that truth is "what I see clearly and distinctly" became the most important battle of new and consistent intellectualism against the bogus intellectualization of the twentieth century.

In the twentieth century, common sense has ceased to be such an effective weapon against the new attacks coming from the new Hobbesian Kingdom of Darkness because this new Kingdom presents itself at first as a realm of reason.

Reason, therefore, must be strengthened by the new theory of argumentation and reasonable solutions must be pluralistic. The New Rhetoric is aware that many people take for granted as obvious and rational what really needs to be proved. They accept traditional ideas although circumstances have changed radically.

Formal logic does not question the premises it is given, while the New Rhetoric, on the other hand, is critical of everything. It does not take anything for granted, it does not accept without question anything that was established in the past; it rejects all explicit or implicit assumptions, premises, and propositions, compelling people to cut to the roots of common-sense itself, to the facts, and truths, themselves.

From the standpoint of the theory of argumentation, facts designate what has been agreed upon by a given audience as incontrovertible.[27] But a "fact"

---

[26] *Ibid.*, p. 25.

can cease to be a fact either because doubts have been raised about it among the given public or because the original public has expanded and the new members have come to question what for others was uncontestable.[28]

Does this imply that facts are completely subjective? The problem is that rhetorical debate is little concerned with the narrow problems to dispel all doubts. It is impossible for example, to find any ultimate criterion to support a political party, which would be able to confirm something to be a fact independently of a listener's attitude.[29]

A fact without the support of argumentation behind it cannot survive by itself in a world of dissenters. A fact does not possess its own vitality, its power to survive autonomously.

All these observations concerning "facts" apply to "truth," albeit in a more complex way.[30]

Rhetorical argumentation never concludes; it is like Heraclitus' river: you cannot step into the same river twice. And truth, although ever-changing, still remains something tangible and applicable, because it is continuously questioned in the endless dialogue of unlimited audiences. Heraclitus observed: "Opposition is good . . . everything originates in strife . . . hidden harmony is better than surface harmony."[31]

Rhetoric is an instrument for establishing the true, hidden connections which lie under the surface. Rhetoric always reminds us that the best emerges "out of differents"[32]

Are we condemned to eternal doubt and unrest? "In changing, it rests . . ." and that "which tends to destruction . . . is called concord and peace."[33] Such is one of the pre-Aristotelian wells of rhetoric. They all determine the intrinsic link between the New Rhetoric and democratic pluralism: there is nothing perfect, no order can pretend to be, no social group or party has a monopoly on absolute wisdom or knowledge.

The New Rhetoric constitutes a philosophical and methodo-logical basis for the democratic concept of pluralism. And vice versa: pluralism leads to the theory of argumentation and needs its support for its own existence. Theory and methodology are inseparable from it. These general methodological and philosophical considerations have their direct impact on the philosophy of law, politics, and morality.

---

[27] Ibid., p. 67.

[28] Ibid., pp. 67–68.

[29] Ibid., p. 68.

[30] Ibid., pp. 68–69. What is the difference between facts and truths? From the standpoint of argumentation, it is a relative difference. "The term 'facts' is generally used to designate objects of precise, limited agreement, whereas the term 'truth' is preferably applied to more complex systems relating to connections between facts."

[31] Heraclitus, "Fragments" 46, 47, in Milton C. Nahm, *Selections from Early Greek Philosophy* (New York: Appleton-Century Crofts, 1964).

[32] Ibid., p. 46.

[33] Ibid., p. 83.

CHAPTER III

The New Rhetoric and Dialectics

1. PRELIMINARY REMARKS

Chaim Perelman's New Theory of Argumentation has become an indispensable continuation of the dialectical method, while dialectics is the foundation and the nervous system of the New Rhetoric. The New Rhetoric is the long sought focus which adds new vitality to traditional dialectics and pushes it to new phases of creativity and development.

Dialectics and rhetoric have their own histories. It may even be desirable to assess rhetorical thinking in the historical development of dialectical philosophy and methodology, and vice versa. Our purpose here is only to examine the two highest stages in the evolution of these philosophies: dialectics as developed by Hegel and rhetoric as reborn and developed by Perelman.

In the last sixty years there was a large and influential group of philosophers who contended that it was Marx and eventually Lenin who developed the Hegelian dialectical method and that Marx and Lenin truly represent the pinnacle of dialectics. Indeed Marx and Lenin sought to apply dialectical methodology to assist their own philosophy, political economy, and ideology; they did not however add any new methodological dimension to Hegel's dialectical categories. Even if they made some small contributions there is no duty to waste space on minutiae.

Marx himself wrote that although his dialectic method was the "direct opposite" of Hegel's having turned it "right side up again," it was Hegel who was "the first to present its general working form in a comprehensive and conscious manner." Therefore he, Marx, was able and willing to decide openly to avow himself to be "the pupil of that mighty thinker."[1]

These contentions of Marx should not be regarded as excessively modest: Marx used the Hegelian method in his own way, but did not (if he wished to do so at all) develop this methodology.

Hegel analyzed the following basic categories of dialectics in the classic way, unsurpassed to the present day: contradictions in their antagonisms and

---

[1] Karl Marx, *Capital*, (Chicago: Charles H. Kerr & Co., 1921) vol. 1, p. 25.

25

unit; the real nature and the thinking as *"werden"* (becoming); quantity and quality; necessity and freedom; chance and laws; essence and appearances; substance and form; negation and continuation.

Although Hegel's conception of "the idea" as the demiurgos of the real world is a kind of objective idealism he made a special contribution in analyzing the dialectic of reality and its reflection in the mirror of the mind: the dialectics of the general and particular, of the categories of thinking as stages of apprehending and mastering the world.

To compare dialectics and rhetoric can be properly done by comparing Hegel's dialectical method and the Rhetoric revived and elaborated by Chaim Perelman.

2. DIALECTIC AND RHETORIC ON CONTRADICTIONS AND COMMON SENSE

Rhetorical debate is the means of approaching truth in a world where "everything originates in strife" (Fr. 46), because "war is common to all" (Fr. 62), it is "the father and king of all things"[2] (Fr. 44). Strife (or war – Heraclitus usually uses these two notions in the same sense) is even the source of harmony and justice.

The concept of contradictions is the point of departure of any "materialistic" or "idealistic" dialectics. It is the "soul" of both dialectics and rhetoric alike. This concept is also the foundation of Hegelian logic, conceived in its broadest sense.

Thoughts which do not reflect the complexity of the strife and antagonism are, according to Hegel, "the familiar forms of thought," but they are only, as he wrote in the Preface to the second edition of *The Science of Logic*, – *die leblosen Knochen eines Skeletts*[3] (the lifeless bones of a skeleton). The history of thought is connected with the history of language, and every step in the development of language, being a product of "subjective dialectics," simultaneously becomes an instrument in the further evolution of dialectical thinking. Hegel welcomes the fact that there are words that have *entgegensetzte Bedeutungen*, which means they are not simply different, but they express "opposing meanings".[4]

Every step in the development of our knowledge means new discoveries of contradictions which must be reflected in our language and in the wholeness of subjective dialectics.

The distinction between empirical observation and intellectual reflection (thinking) is relative. This distinction is theoretical rather than practical. But

---

[2] All the quotations of the Fragments (Fr.) of Heraclitus are from: Milton C. Nahm. *Selections from Early Greek Philosophy*, fourth edition (Appleton-Century-Crofts. New York. 1964).
[3] G. W. Fr. Hegel., Collected Works. Berlin, 1983. vol. III *The Science of Logic*, p. ii.
[4] Hegel, *op. cit.*, p. 12.

it is important to notice that according to the rhetorical viewpoint we are exposed to the danger of error in every area, at every stage of the process of acquiring knowledge.

In the sphere of thinking and its relationship to the empirical data, we are constantly exposed to the danger of over- or underestimating the empirical data, and over- or underestimating "common sense." Hegel calls denials based solely on common sense *"eine pöbelhafte Widerlegung"*.[5] He referred here to the famous proof by Diogenes of movement (against the Eleatics): he walked up and down.

Indeed, Diogenes' proof is far from vulgar; he used it against philosophical adversaries who employed intellectual tricks to deny the undeniable: the mere existence of movement. What is *pöbelhaft* ("vulgar") depends not only on the quality of the arguments, but also on the circumstances in which they are made, including the perceptions and intelligence of the audience, the behavior and the means used by the adversary whom one wants either to defeat or to persuade.

The use of common sense is usually ridiculous whenever one wants to use it to refute more complicated theses derived from scientific research. It was after all "common sense", which was misused in order to prove that the earth does not and cannot move. The adversaries of Copernicus and Galileo Galilei were for a long time very successful in their appeals to "common sense." Thereby proving that "common sense," if it is not submitted to rigorous rhetorical criticism, can be as abused as any other category.

The rhetorical and dialectical concepts of common sense are indeed identical. Hegel wrote:

> This is the ordinary view of so-called common sense, which holds fast to the evidence of the *senses* and to customary ideas and expressions.[6]

From the generic and epistemological viewpoint, "sound, common sense" is a creation of two processes: sense observations combined with the most common, widespread, simple and simplistic ideas, persuasions (and prejudices) of a given society. These ideas have been historically and socially formed, they are inherited from the previous generations, therefore they have the power and respect of tradition, of an alleged self-evidence, of a Cartesian clarity and distinctness.

The rudimentary law of dialectical and rhetorical thinking requires that in order to understand one cannot stop at the surface; one must not accept the results of the first glance, mere sense observation, but one should penetrate deeper under the surface of phenomena.

---

[5] "A vulgar denial".

[6] Hegel, *op cit.*, p. 337–338 Justice Oliver W. Holmes made a similar observation: "The jurists who believe in natural law seem to me to be in that naive state of mind that accepts what has been familiar and accepted by them and their neighbors as something that must be accepted by all men everywhere" – in Oliver Wendell Holmes, *Collected Legal Papers* (New York: Peter Smith, 1952), p. 312.

Hegel simply stated: " . . . *was bekannt ist, ist darum noch nicht erkannt*".[7]
Indeed it was Heraclitus who was the first who observed: "Learning of many
things does not teach one to have understanding . . . " (Fr. 16); many do not
think about the things they experience, nor do they know the things they
learn, but they think they know (Fr. 5). We are misled when we believe in
our senses ("eyes and ears are bad witnesses for men" – Fr. 4) and we are
misled when we uncritically mistrust them, because then we are like fools who
when "they hear, are like deaf men", who "though present they are not there"
(Fr. 3). Why is it so? Because "nature loves to hide" (Fr. 10) and it does not
easily reveal its secrets.

Dialectics is a method that holds that external phenomena (forms) hide
internal, essential, laws. Rhetoric is the instrument to unveil the essence from
under the misleading forms. What is the essence? According to dialectics,
the essence is the contradictions composed into unity.

Participants in rhetorical dialogue reveal and stress various elements of
internal incompatibilities. When the observers and the participants in the
dialogue see those various elements exposed and draw their own conclusions, they are in disagreement. Who is right? Who is wrong? It can happen
– this is one of the principal points of Perelman's works – that both are right,
although their conclusions may be contradictory.

How is that possible? Is it not against "common sense", against Cartesian
dogma and the principles of the formal logic? It is possible from the dialectical and rhetorical viewpoints because participants in the dialogue are
observing and selecting (every observation is a selection) various real aspects
(elements) of the same infinitely various reality (every fragment of reality is
also epistemologically and dialectically infinite, as we have already observed).

The purpose of rhetorical dialogue is not merely an endless, although
enlightening, discussion, but reasonable choices and decisions. Because of these
practical purposes, rhetorical dialogue has to put temporary restrictions on
the infinite dialectical depths and many-sidedness; it recommends acceptance
of preliminary results and approves practical applications.

From this point of view rhetorical dialogue is like Hegelian idea, which
while being "the universal reality," is at the same time "a process at rest".[8]

This rest is only relative, because it is only a springboard and a means
for continuation.

3. THE NEW RHETORIC AND THE DIALECTICS OF PLURALISM

The New Rhetoric is by no means a mere reduplication of Aristotle's works.
The New Rhetoric constitutes the Hegelian *Aufhebung* of Aristotle's rhetoric.

---

[7]   Hegel, *op. cit.*, p. 13, "What is known, is not on that account understood."
[8]   *Hegel's Lectures on The History of Philosophy* (London: Routledge and Kegan Paul.
New York: The Humanities Press, 1974) vol 1, p. 293.

It is at once a continuation and a negation of that rhetoric. The novelty of Perelman's theory is chiefly his introduction and elaboration of the notion of "audience" and pluralism.

Perelman enlarged the Aristotelian theory of dialectical reasoning and its conception as a generalized rhetoric or general theory of argumentation. This theory includes not only the theory of the more or less incompetent audience but it includes audiences of all kinds. Even the most specialized.

Another new and thoroughly expounded element in it is the elaboration of the rhetorical discourse in close connection with politics, jurisprudence and the philosophy of pluralism. The rhetorical notion of pluralism is a milestone in a genuine philosophical sense which leads to answers to many of the traditional problems of the philosophy of law and politics, without recourse to fiction or mythology. Bentham's dream of the purification of the theory and practice of law by expunging the then prevalent legal fictions has at long last been accomplished.

In the essay "The New Rhetoric: A Theory of Practical Reasoning", Perelman tells about his own intellectual evolution and throws some light on a part of the way which he has traveled. His first study of justice was published in 1945. One of the principles he in 1945 adhered to is that one cannot draw an "ought" from an "is", that there is an unsurmountable barrier between judgments of fact and those of value, between *sein* and *sollen*. Hence the conclusion: every normative system is arbitrary and logically indeterminate; it cannot be subjected to any rational criticism, it is incompatible with "formal necessity" and "experiential universality".

He was deeply dissatisfied with this conclusion, and in this frame of mind he asked himself: " . . . is there a logic of value judgments that makes it possible for us to reason about values instead of making them depend solely on irrational choice, based on interest, passion, prejudice and myth? Recent history has shown abundantly the sad excess to which such an attitude can lead"[9]

Perelman was unable to accept the concept that ends themselves cannot be subjected to reasonable analysis, but was, instead, deeply convinced that we are not condemned to such a limited choice as for example between A. J. Ayer's view (*Language, Truth and Logic*) or G. E. Moore's (*Principia Ethica*). Nor could he accept existentialist subjectivism, as has been stressed

He finally found a way to solve this dilemma.

The result of the new investigations is documented in his book *The New Rhetoric* and in subsequent works. The old classical pre-socratic and Socratic rhetorical and dialectical tradition was revived.

But, as we have already mentioned, what is reborn always has original elements and operates in a new manner under circumstances very different from those of its genesis.

There is no doubt that the New Rhetoric was born as a result of new

---

[9] Ch. Perelman "The New Rhetoric: A Theory of Practical Reasoning", in *The Great Ideas Today* 1970, Encyclopaedia Britannica, Chicago, 1970, p. 280.

practical and theoretical needs. Traditional philosophies were unable to answer the new questions. On the other hand, people were pressed to make reasonable decisions because new waves of irrationalism have also been emerging in the well-established western democracies.

Chaim Perelman was directly influenced by his teacher and mentor, the eminent Belgian philosopher, Eugène Dupréel, who sought to create a counterweight to the classical philosophies which he referred to as absolutistic. He did this in his work on the Sophists. Perelman continued the ideas of Dupréel, but went beyond him.

The philosophers, argued Dupréel, seek truth and values which they try to impose on society; truths and values, have one feature in common: monism.

To the classic concept of monism Dupréel opposed his own concept of pluralism. Perelman, like Dupréel, spoke about pluralism from various viewpoints: axiology, sociology, politics, science (including the field of Academia). Perelman continued Dupréel's initiative and criticized classical rationalism for neglecting the social aspects of knowledge which was one of the intellectual reasons why the rationalists had never been able to reach an understanding of the problem of the *diversity and plurality of minds*

Perelman drew some of his basic philosophical and rhetorical conclusions from Dupréel's assertion that every informal idea or theory is imperfect. Practically speaking, this means that every program, every order, every mind or group of minds, can be improved. If they were perfect, if the achievement of perfection were at all possible, then pluralism would be indefensible.

In this way Perelman reached the conclusion of the "natural" imperfection of every form of society. The same conclusion was reached by Heraclitus and Hegel, although they proceeded from another point of departure: concept of eternal contradictions, "fire", development, and negation.

Perelman drew from Depréel's premises such philosophical and political conclusions which were never reached in such a clear form by his predecessors: the creative role of dialogue.

The way the plurality of imperfect minds operates is through dialogue. Whatever the form of the dialogue may be, it is indispensable to understand and to be understood. Dialogue is a nourishment, a stimulant for the mind; it generates intellectual progress and is part of the "subjective dialectics" itself. The isolated man must be even more imperfect than a man who is a member of the community or "plurality of minds". Dialogue, conceived as the interrelation between speaker and audience, was introduced by the New Theory of Argumentation from pluralistic considerations and became a central focus in The New Rhetoric.

Perelman developed Dupréel's idea that progress itself creates new problems and hindrances. The progress created by industrial techniques was a source of new disorders, new difficulties and dangers, because militarist imperialism and the preponderance of economic power produced excesses. Perelman saw the new threats to freedom, and therefore his rhetorical pluralism is consciously and deliberately opposed to all forms of totalitarianism which are, philosophically, the final uniformity, *Gleichschaltung*, dogmatism, a belief in final truth and absolute value, a belief in the notion of a unique order without inherent conflicts. Perelman argued that the central philosophical and political problem is that in social life we encounter conflicts.[10] Here he followed Dupréel, that what is most difficult and essential is "the search for means to moderate these conflicts, temper the antagonisms through a social technique centered on the notion of convention. Convention results from an accord of minds freely instituting a common order; diverse conventions allow for the institution of multiple orders."[11]

Pluralism assumes that the "best" life, the incarnation of Reason will never be achieved; pluralism always seeks improvement through compromises, accommodations, and synthesis; it is rooted in the methodological significance of the "unclear idea".[12] All these phenomena embody one common feature: reasonableness.

Once we conclude that pluralism must seek accommodation and compromise, then we must also conclude that individuals should not push their interests and convictions too far: they should be moderate and prudent. People can live reasonably, as individuals, as members of a group, and as citizens of the state, and in all three capacities at the same time, without endangering the foundation of the social edifice. They can live together in equilibrium, symbiotically, each person pursuing a way of life acceptable to all. Every individual can preserve a certain amount of freedom and individuality. Under any unitary, absolutistic order, pretending to represent absolute values, freedom consists only in the freedom to conform, Perelman wrote. Absolutistic orders impose conformity and every imposed conformity is intrinsically opposed to creative initiative and genuine freedom of choice. Freedom can be enjoyed and exercised only in a differentiated, pluralistic society where the individual can enter into a multiplicity of allegiances and at the same time transcend every group of which he is a member.

An original, pre-social liberty of the "noble" savage or the anguished existentialist never existed. What exists in reality, if the notion of freedom is to have any sense, is "the freedom of the man who liberates himself from purely social imperatives and is capable of elaborating a moral ideal which gives meaning to his life, an assured direction to his action. It is the freedom of conscious man, who is not the toy of external forces."[13] Consequently, it is misleading to say that man is born free. Freedom is not an attribute of man, it emerges in action. "It belongs only to the one who takes in hand the direction of his life and is completely responsible for his acts.[14]

[10]   Perelman, "Dialectik und Dialog", *Hegel Jahrbuch 1970*, Anton Hain, Meisenheim am Glan, 1971, p. 19.
[11]   Perelman. *À propos d'Eugène Dupréel, Contribution à un portrait philosophique, Revue Internationale de Philosophie*, 83–84, p. 230.
[12]   Dupréel wrote a classical essay on the unclear idea and its methodological significance. It was written as a fundamental critique of Descartes' concept of the clear and distinct idea.
[13]   Perelman, *À propos d'Eugène Dupréel*, p. 231.

Perelman approached dialectics of freedom another way: this time the theory that freedom regarded as comprehened "necessity" is Perelman's point of departure; although it is different from that of Hegel, but the philosophical conclusions are similiar.[15]

Dupréel distinguished between the *critical spirit* and the *dogmatic spirit*. This distinction has an immediate connection with Perelmans's elaboration of rhetoric as the foundation for pluralism.

The dogmatic is characterized by an inclination to reject any criticism or questioning; this spirit serves the purposes of conservative social groups.

The critical spirit is a disposition to respect every truth, known or to be discovered; it favors the opinions of minorities and defends an emerging notion against dogmatic, conservative, entrenched ideas, usually supported by established social groups. A critical mind is individualistic and liberal, whereas the dogmatic person attaches importance to tradition; a traditionalist must be more of a conformist than anyone else.

This is where Perelman diverged from Dupréel. This departure was not, of course, a rejection; it was a new exploration which went deeper into the problem because Perelman took more decisive steps toward dialectics.

He wrote:

Personally, I would accord more importance to a notion which is significant in Dupréel's thought, to which he refers frequently in his philosophy and sociology. This is the *agreement of minds* tied to the problem of persuasion . . . It is curious to state that Dupréel who gave such importance to persuasion and the agreement of minds, who knew Greek philosophy so well . . . did not perceive the importance of rhetoric for his own philosophy or its importance as a technique seeking to bring about an agreement of values . . .[16]

Agreement of minds is a relative unity of different ideas which were united in order to achieve practical, reasonable ends. From the rhetorical viewpoint differences and contradictions are not disruptive; they do not destroy solidarity, but on the contrary, contradictions are the timber which the New Rhetoric uses in order to achieve agreement (but not *Gleichschaltung*) of minds.

The pluralistic concept of the political society, as understood by Perelman, is a logical, rationalistic and reasonable set of conclusions based on the dialectical concept of the perennial strife of contradictions.

---

[14] *Ibid.*, p. 231.

[15] My analysis of the Hegelian-Marxian ideas of freedom, the reader can find in "*Interpretation:*", No 1. vol. 1978 (New York: Queens College Press) and in my *Freedom and Tolerance*, op. cit., pp. 46–65.

[16] Perelman, A propos d'Eugene Dupréel. Contribution a un portrait philosphique, *Review Internationale de Philosophie*, 83–84, p. 236.

4. DIALOGUE IN THE STRUCTURE OF DIALECTICS IN THE NEW RHETORIC

Dialogue is the form and animating spirit of the process of argumentation.

Argumentation is the technique that we use in controversy when we are concerned with criticizing and justifying, objecting and refuting, of asking and giving reasons.

There are two preconditions for the existence of dialogue:
- the interest of a speaker (writer) and an audience in an exchange of ideas,
- freedom of the participants to be candid with one another. People who are afraid to speak their minds to one another can never convince one another.

The concept of audience is crucial in the structure of the New Rhetoric. Audience can be generally defined from the rhetorical viewpoint as "the ensemble of these whom the speaker wishes to influence by his argumentation".[17]

Must the outcome of dialogue necessarily be just, true, socially desirable? No.

At times one tries to persuade one individual. But generally speaking, for socially valid reasons, the point of departure should not be the individual with his specific emotions, prejudices, or idiosyncrasies, but the social group which has combined in itself the *essential* common opinions and interests. The speaker should know what distinguishes one social environment from another; he should understand that the most important factors, from the sociological viewpoint, are: "the social functions exercised by its listeners". Either a speaker (writer) will to adapt himself to his given audience or he will risk antagonizing them. He may even impress many who may be fond of him as a human being and appreciate him as a prominent personality, but who nevertheless reject the cause which he advocates.

It is most important in understanding the art of true rhetoric to know what rhetoric is not. It is not a *scientia male dicendi*. It is not the art of using immoral means for immoral ends. It is not an art which can be used by unscrupulous public relations manipulators who serve dictators, despots, or depraved politicians, prepared to promise everything but intending to deliver nothing. This explains why the New Rhetoric introduced the idea of the universal audience, including the audience of philosophers who can be convinced only by truly acceptable arguments.

During the flow of argumentation free people will sooner or later detect the lies and misrepresentations so necessary to deceivers. One may or may not be persuaded by arguments. When argumentation fails to persuade, that still does not mean that it was unreasonable. Arguments can be rejected by audiences for various reasons, but lies used in a free exchange of arguments can be brought to light sooner than in any other way. There are no guarantees against deception, but the deception will be found out when the interlocutor

---

[17] Perelman, L. Olbrechts-Tyteca, *The New Rhetoric*, p. 19.

is free to think, to speak, to collect material, to investigate the case, when he is free and prepared to take part in the process of argumentation.

The New Rhetoric is meant to be an art of persuasion, of gaining the adherence of normal people who may not be angels, but not scoundrels either.

The New Rhetoric is the art of winning over the minds and adherence of people who may be mistaken, but at least have the good will to commence thinking about an issue. The New Rhetoric is meant to be a Diogenes' lamp for those who travel along a road which is dimly lit, full of hazardous curves, and traversing unknown domains.

The New Rhetoric does not take anything for granted, including Descartes' that truth is what "I see clearly and distinctly."

Descartes requires first doubt and then acceptance as truth, "what I see clearly and distinctly." This requirement was important and progressive in the seventeenth and eighteenth centuries. The official theological teachings presented little which the common minds could see clearly or distinctly. The simplest Cartesian principles of obviousness, of dividing theses into the most simple predicates, of thoroughly reviewing the results, were in their very nature anti-theological. But in the twentieth century the same common sense ceased to be such an effective instrument against new perversions of common sense, both in the industrial democracies and in the totalitarian countries. Why? Because they presented themselves in the categories of logic.

Mass propaganda in a mass society, the "selling" of ideas, of presidents, and even the clergy, tends to channel thoughts into a one track, one-way flow, alleged to be obvious. It is a pseudo "common sense" which, together with blatant irrationalism, has become one of the worst and the most dangerous enemies of reason in modern, industrial democracies.

Rhetoric is a way of overcoming the power of appearances[18], of dogmas, myths, and the "obvious truths" of common sense. The rhetorical flow of arguments, the appeal to an audience and the invitation to it to join in dialogue – these are the tools for criticism of simplistic ideas which remain deeply ingrained in the minds of people who, generally speaking, are rather critical, innovative, and even creative in their professional lives, but are unable or unwilling to apply the same demanding criteria to a many-sided analysis of social and political issues.

The New Rhetoric takes into consideration that the lack of a critical attitude is widespread, that many people take for granted as logical, obvious, and rational, what needs to be proved. They accept traditional concepts at their face value after new circumstances have invalidated them.

In this situation it is traditional logic which can be used to explain, justify, and rationalize every "being," every thing that is. Formal logic does not question the premises, while Rhetoric on the other hand, examines every-

---

[18] " . . . not every appearance would be true: for an appearance is an appearance to someone, so he who states that all appearances are true makes things relative". Aristotle, *Metaphysics* 1011a, 19–21, p. 69.

thing. It does not take anything for granted, it rejects all the explicit or implicit assumptions, premises, and propositions, compelling people to cut down into the roots of common-sense itself.

Two notions are especially pertinent to the problem of the relationship between the New Rhetoric and the democratic concept of pluralism: facts, and truths.

No matter what we may discuss or when we may discuss it, be it the problem of opinions, convictions, or persuasion, we sooner or later revert to the basic question posed by Pontius Pilate: "And what is truth?"

"Truth is infinite" – writes Hegel. From the dialectical viewpoint truth is not just a statement based on the Aristotelian *adaequatio rei et intellectus*, but truth is a *process of adaequatio*, of *erkennen*, of understanding, knowing, of the intellectual penetration into the substance, the world, nature, humanity, every piece of matter and every social relation, which are infinite; therefore truth conceived as a dialectical process of reflecting upon the objectivity, performed by the subjective mind, is also infinite. To limit truth would be, in Hegel's opinion, to "deny" it. The forms of thought (*Denkformen*) originate from substance but they are distinct from substance, and they are incapable of "embracing" the "whole truth." Therefore every truth is only partial. But partial *truth* is really *truth*, because it embraces a part of the absolute truth which mankind will achieve in eternity.[19] If the absolute truth will only be achieved in eternity, one might argue that it will never be achieved. The little change in this sentence signifies the difference between the philosophy of absolute relativism (if its existence is possible!) and the philosophy of relativity at the given stage of the evolution of truth.

The knowledge which mankind possesses at every stage of its development consists of the infinite sum of relative truths. The given stage of human knowledge encompasses a sum of partial *objective* truths and this knowledge can be instrumental for practical activity.

In one of his less known passages on the relationship between thought and action, Hegel wrote that "intelligent and conscious action" is a result of the fact that an intelligent man, in contradiction to a savage, distinguishes himself from his environment, from the "immediate unity" with nature and society and confronts the "web" of categories.

"In this web, strong knots are formed now and then, which are foci of the arrest and direction of its . . . life and consciousness".[20]

The intellectual categories constructed by men are stages of knowing the world. They are the focal points (called by Hegel "foci") in the web, which enable people to understand nature and to master it. Thus we return, proceeding in the dialectical way, to the great Baconian observation that in order to become a master, man must be a minister. But a minister is not a passive servant in the process of cognition; he acts and uses every available partial truth for

[19]   Hegel, *The Science of Logic, op. cit.*, p. 19.
[20]   Hegel, *op. cit.*, p. 18.

his practical purposes. During practical activity man derives the "categories" – he does not "expose" them, but develops *das Denken in seiner Notwendigkeit*[21] which simply means: the evolution of thought consists in the discoveries of the unknown laws of nature, of unknown associations, relations, and interdependencies. But the road from relative truth does not necessarily lead to a higher, more refined truth. It can also serve as "instruments of error and sophistry."[22] This is the real danger to which every relative truth exposes us and which we should try consciously to avoid. These is a method of diminishing the real danger of errors: free argumentation which exposes ambiguity, and awareness of the "natural," "innate," complexity of every "category," "law," and "course of action."

Rhetorical "truth" is not the antithesis of Aristotelian "metaphysical truth". It puts the latter into its place; it does not dethrone it; it shows its limits by pointing out that it is not the final end, but it is an end which necessarily serves as a means to achieve further ends.

Dialectics by its own virtue calls for free examination and attempts to overthrow all ruling gods. Dialectics calls for a rhetorical dialogue because this is the only way to preserve its existence. Dialectics and rhetoric represent two sides of a democratic method of research in a politically free environment. Dialogue presupposes that the participants are not inhibited, otherwise an appeal to critical reasoning and knowledge of contradictions would be pointless.

Dialectics and rhetoric complement each other; they both need political democracy, while democracy can not exist and develop without them.

Let us return once more to the rhetorical concept of fact.

Remembering these brief reminders of the Aristotelian concept of truth, let us analyze rhetorical epistemology.

From the standpoint of argumentation, "facts" are certain types of data based on objective reality; "facts" designate what has been agreed upon by a given audience as incontrovertible.

But it follows that no statement can be assured of definitively enjoying this status because the agreement can always be called in question later and one of the parties to the debate may refuse to qualify his opponent's affirmation as a fact.[23]

How is it that a fact can cease to be a fact? There are two ways in which this can happen – doubts have to be raised within the given audience; or the given audience has been expanded and the new audience questions what was incontestable to the former.[24]

This does not imply that "facts" are completely subjective, that they depend completely on the agreement of the participants in a debate. Rhetorical debate

21   Hegel, *op. cit.*, p. 22.
22   Hegel, *op. cit.*, p. 20.
23   C. Perelman, *The New Rhetoric*, p. 67.
24   *Ibid.*, p. 67–68.

does not deal with the narrow problems of the natural sciences where one can dispel all doubts. From the standpoint of argumentation it is the power of an argument that has to influence and persuade the audience to support, for example, this or that political party or the continuation or discontinuation of an expensive weapons system. There is no ultimate criterion which can make something a fact independently of a listener's attitude.

Nevertheless, we may recognize that there are certain conditions favoring this agreement, rendering the fact easily defensible in the face of an opponent's mistrust or ill will. This will be the case, in particular, when there is agreement on conditions for verification ... Accepted facts may be either observed facts – this is perhaps the case for most premises – or supposed, agreed facts, facts that are possible or probable. There is thus a considerable mass of elements that is compelling to the hearer or which the speaker strives to make compelling.[25]

Facts become facts in the process of argumentation, when they are accepted and agreed upon as facts. But their lives may be brief during the course of argumentation because they may be challenged at any time by other facts and must be defended against them. A fact without the power of reason behind it cannot survive by itself in our competitive world. A fact cannot live autonomously.

A fact in argumentation is nothing more than a subjective reflection of the objective reality so long as it is not undermined by the counterarguments of its adversaries.

All observations concerning facts are applicable to "truths," which is a more complex problem.

What is the difference between facts and truths? From the standpoint of argumentation the difference is relative. "The term 'facts' is generally used to designate objects of precise, limited, agreement, whereas the term 'truth' is preferably applied to more complex systems relating to connections between facts".[26]

Philosophical discussions concerning the relationship between facts, truths, and their theories are too numerous to explore here. Nevertheless, the above distinction is helpful with regard to the theory of argumentation and is legitimized through the purpose intended, its practical application in discourse. "It is also possible to so conceive their relationship that the statement of a fact is truth and that any truth enunciates a fact."[27]

We return to the fundamentals: the link between Aristotelian *Metaphysics* (with its theory of truth), and Aristotle's *Rhetoric* (as the theory of argumentation) which was re-established by the New Rhetoric, namely, that truth is connected with the "objective reality," with its assessment, perception, and ultimately, with the practical activity which dialectically influences reality.

---

[25] C. Perelman, *op. cit.*, p. 68.
[26] *Ibid.*, pp. 68–69.
[27] Perelman, *op. cit.*, p. 69.

The theory of argumentation with its discursive concept of facts and truths is wholly dialectical: it holds nothing sacred, nothing established, nothing taken for granted. And yet is indispensable in the search for truth, progress, beauty, and human freedom. Eternal values (with their everchanging content) can be founded only on the rock of doubt and contradiction.

We have now established the element linking the New Rhetoric with pre-Aristotelian and Aristotelian contributions. The new theory of argumentation goes beyond Aristotle because among other things it was able to consciously to absorb the pre-Aristotelian Sophists: the teachings of Gorgias and Protagoras were re-evaluated by the tradition of Dupréel.

Western culture has generally held that any conclusions reached by human thought must be a personal and subjective conviction, that every conclusion must be examined and must be the result of an investigation, not merely blind belief.

Such is also the ideal of rhetorical discourse. Everything that falls into the stream of argumentation changes its meaning and place in the system of thought, invading the substance of the system itself. Rhetorical discourse reshapes the essence and the reformed essence itself shines through and becomes more general yet particular at the same time. It becomes more distant but it embraces more.

Rhetorical argumentation never ceases; it does not know stops, breaks, or pauses. It flows continually, like Heraclitus' river. Every truth is continuously questioned in a search for contradictions and harmony.[28]

According to dialectics and the New Rhetoric, "the fairest harmony comes out of differences".[29]

The intrinsic link between rhetorical methodology, dialectics, and pluralism is the premise that there is nothing perfect; no political party or church can have a monopoly upon absolute wisdom and knowledge.

The New Rhetoric constitutes a philosophical and methodological basis for pluralism. It is an instrument of analysis and synthesis, being a creative social activity.

The ideal of pluralism as conceived by the New Rhetoric is diametrically opposed to the philosophy and methodology of scepticism or relativism, as understood by Hans Kelsen, for instance.

In his famous considerations about Pontius Pilate, Kelsen argued that the act of washing hands was a truly and consistently democratic act because there is no valid criterion to distinguish between the value of the life of a convicted criminal and that of a man who identified himself as the messenger of truth. Let us examine this approach.

---

[28] Heraclitus, "Fragments" 46, 47, in Milton C. Nahm, *Selections from Early Greek Philosophy* (New York, Appleton-Century Crofts, 1964).
[29] *Ibid.*, p. 46.

5. THE RHETORICAL AND DIALECTICAL MEANING OF COMPROMISE AND SCEPTICISM

Hans Kelsen wrote that once we accept the relativistic concept that in the realm of values truth cannot be known, that everything is relative (except relativity), then we must also accept as justifiable the behaviour and decision of the cynical Roman governor. It may be that an intellectually consistent, logical, and rationalistic skeptic and relativist could agree with Kelsen's conclusions. But they are not acceptable to the New Rhetoric or to pluralism based on argumentation.

The New Rhetoric does not reject all moral, political, social, legal, and philosophical ideals as senseless or worthless. It only subjects these ideals, their interpretation, and application to endless critical scrutiny. Rhetoric does not tell people to stop having their conflicts because everything is equally bad or good. It only teaches people the old Roman wisdom: *quidquid agis – prudenter agas et respice finem.* Be reasonable – whatever you do and look at the end; whatever you decide – subject it to dialectical criticism and argumentation. Look beyond that end of your nose – as the old Polish saying advises.

According to rhetorical methodology solutions may be worse or better with every development of society: with the advent of new arguments what was worse can become better (or at least seems so), and vice versa. Even more, one may find a better third, fourth, or fifth solution, because we, our lives, our social and political systems are not confined to the apodictic either-or, take it or leave it, love it or hate it.

The method of Rhetoric is against dogmatism: it is for pluralism, for democracy, for unlimited intellectual freedom.

By its very nature dialectics is critical and revolutionary, wrote Karl Marx. But experience shows that even dialectics can be used for anti-progressive, non-humanistic ends. Let us only refer to the three philosophers already mentioned.

Heraclitus used his allegedly obscure dialectics to criticize a newly established anti-aristocratic government. In his own opinion it was a government of the mob and was doomed. Hegel's absolute idea has been in constant dialectical motion but it "returned" to itself in the form of the Prussian monarchy of Frederick William II and therefore no further development was necessary or possible. Marx and Engels criticized Hegel's philosophy as suffering from an incurable internal contradiction between its revolutionary method and its reactionary theoretical system but they too fell into an old trap. They transformed the laws of evolution and revolution, the law of negation and of the negation of negation into dogmas and started to make non-dialectical predictions about the advent of the communist society in which the contradiction between social needs and the means of consumption would disappear. When these contradictions which they themselves regarded as dialectical generators of energy, invention, productivity, and progress disappear, what will replace them to "drive" human development forward? Stalin and Zhdanov answered that the new force for progress would be the moral unity of the classless society, reviving in this way, with the help of dialectics, the anti-dialectical and well exorcised ghost of objective idealism. What was meant by this "moral unity" and how it was to be fostered and preserved has been demonstrated by the Soviet bureaucracy.

History has shown that dialectics has been used not only as a weapon of criticism, but also as a means to impose absolute ideals and dogmas, often in a hidden, perverse manner.

The dialectical travesty of Hegel and Marx-Lenin-Stalin-Mao is especially appealing to less critical minds, because they proclaim a "milder" form of absolute ideals.

Their ideals were proclaimed "absolute" however only at a particular stage of the historical process, during the dictatorship of the proletariat. Although this necessity is temporary, it is nevertheless "unavoidable," a forward-looking person should be reasonable and support the Prussian monarchy or the Soviet or Chinese dictatorships.

The New Rhetoric, and especially Professor Perelman himself, in his essays, lectures, debates, and innumerable oral explanations, challenged the mere concept of necessity in the Hegelian- Marxian interpretation.

This is one of the basic differences between dialectics and the New Rhetoric. According to the latter, decisions should be made on the basis of rhetorically accepted premises, "facts," and "truths." The "ideals" and "ends" approved by the given audience, or nation, should not be treated as absolute values, but everything concerning them should be debatable and debated at every stage. The New Rhetoric does not recognize any "political mandate" given to a president or parliament indefinitely and without any reservations or conditions.

Rhetorical thought is against all kinds of conservatism: conservatism of the real status quo and conservatism of ideals and alleged necessities.

Rhetorical thought rejects as ominous the scheme of the "negation of negation," because rhetoric tries to single out every element of progress, every grain of humanistic development. Rejection ("negation") of the obsolete forms should take place as an element of a rhetorically accepted development supported by society.

Rhetorical thought does not reject the notions of quality and quantity but it does not attach any mystical meaning to the dialectical law of quantitative and qualitative changes. What in the field of society, politics, and morality is a "new" or an "old" quality cannot be absolutely determined *a priori*, but must be decided in the course of rhetorical dialogue.

The same reasoning applies to other dialectical categories such as essence and appearance, substance and form, negation and continuation, laws and chance, general and particular.

All these categories can be useful, but they can also be converted into tools of dogmatism and absolutism. They can be helpful only so long as they are debatable and are only means to assist in acquiring knowledge rather than independent sources of wisdom.

These are the principal reasons for our assertion that the New Rhetoric does not cut itself off from the various dialectical traditions. Rhetoric can serve today as a more precise tool in the perennial struggle for humanistic progress. Rhetoric finds desirable and undesirable elements everywhere and helps to struggle for new solutions. It is against all types of radicalism, because every radicalism overlooks or disregards the elements of the existing reality and established philosophy which are, or could still be, beneficial to society.

Rhetoric favors reasonable compromises, not to halt the evolution of social relations, legal systems, or political institutions, but to foster this evolution by critically rejecting what has become obsolete and critically defending what is developing or should be allowed to be born and to live.

For the New Rhetoric, compromise is not an unprincipled, cowardly solution, but on the contrary:

> At the theoretical level. It is the compromise solution to incompatibilities which calls for the greatest effort and is most difficult to justify because it requires a reconstruction of reality. On the other hand, once it is established, once the concepts have been dissociated and restructured, compromise tends to appear as the inescapable solution and to react on the aggregate of concepts into which it is inserted.[30]

Compromise is an instrument and a generator of further evolution, because it is a result of the conflict of opposing forces; compromise does not pretend to resolve all incompatibilities forever, on the contrary, it creates new sources of struggle and motion. Compromise itself is a result of the pluralistic society. Conscious, reasonable compromises help to promote the development of democratic institutions. Rhetorical compromise is a temporary unity of negotiable means and ends.

The New Rhetoric is an indispensable instrument which leads from relativity, from the universality and particularity of the endless process of thinking, of *erkennen*, to reasonable decision making and practical activity based on conscious choice. The dialectical way of acquiring knowledge, the infinite process of *erkennen*, does not know any stops or unshakeable principles: people are not purely contemplative creatures, they are primarily acting and active beings, who therefore must rely, at least for some time, on certain accepted and agreed principles. This acceptance constitutes the spiritual foundation on whose basis people can continue to act. They are able to persuade others and can themselves be persuaded. No one can be persuaded who does not accept certain premises which must also be known to and accepted by the other party. This is an elementary rule of dialogue.

In order to move forward even the most critical and innovative minds have to accept rules or "axioms" which they can afterwards either modify or

---

[30] Perelman, Olbrechts-Tyteca, *The New Rhetoric*, p. 415.

even reject. Rhetorical agreement in a given audience is not a contract for mutual convenience lacking principle, but an essential element on the way to reaching desirable ends. This is a reasonable result of previous experience and knowledge. Such agreement could never be reached if the members of the audience had no common experience, education, culture, knowledge, and – last but not least – a common interest. It is worth noting that a similar observation was made by Albert Einstein in his lecture, "Geometry and Experience", delivered before the Prussian Academy of Sciences in 1921:

"For it cannot occasion surprise that different persons should arrive at the same logical conclusions when they have *agreed upon* (emphasis supplied) the fundamental propositions (axioms) as well as the methods by which other propositions are to be deduced therefrom".[31]

In the flow of contradictions, research, and arguments, there must be an agreement (of course, temporary) upon fundamental propositions.

Hence an agreement in the dialectical process and in a rhetorical dispute is stripped of its conventional relativity and subjectivity; it is an objective and necessary point of departure for further argumentation, for rational decision making and for reasonable practical choices.

Being a theory and methodology, the New Rhetoric serves as a down-to-earth instrument for bridging the gap between dialectical thinking and practical activity.

The rhetorical method is an instrument which helps to "aufheben", to negate and to continue, to overcome and to reinstate the relativity of every conclusion for immediate practical purposes. And when the need is over, it is the rhetorical approach which undermines the solid stuff which it helped to create.

When comprehended in its complex, dynamic interrelationship with dialectics, the New Rhetoric becomes an integral part of subjective dialectics. So far as the latter is a reflection of objective dialectics, the New Rhetoric is a sort of general knowledge (understood here as an *allgemeines Erkenntnis*) of nature and society. Epistemology is not after all absolutely separated from ontology, but constitutes its other side.

Rhetorical methodology is consistently pluralistic. In the evaluation of reality, in the criticism of ideas and ideals, in acceptance and in rejection. For the first time pluralism has found a methodology which it previously lacked; dialectics has a fulcrum for its infinite self-creation, and contradictions can be expressed and overcome in a non-offensive way.

---

[31]   Albert Einstein, *Ideas and Opinions*, New York: Dell Publishing Co., 1973, p. 227.

CHAPTER IV

The Rhetorical View of Power and Authority

As applied to politics, the New Rhetoric can be described as a theory to preserve legitimate authority, as against usurpation.

The distinction between authority and power is not generally accepted in the field of political science. Nevertheless, there are traditions which call for such a distinction.

Perelman himself was influenced by John Stuart Mills' study, "On Liberty." He refers especially to the following:

> The struggle between Liberty and Authority is the most conspicuous feature in the portions of history with which we are earliest familiar, particularly in that of Greece, Rome, and England. . . . By Liberty was meant the protection against the tyranny of the political rulers. The rulers . . . constituted of a governing One, or a governing tribe, or caste, who derived their authority from inheritance or conquest, who, at all events, did not hold it at the pleasure of the governed, and whose supremacy men did not venture, perhaps did not desire, to contest, whatever precaution might be taken against its oppressive exercise.[1]

It is not by chance that Perelman referred to Mill's classic "On Liberty." He was not only influenced by Mill's reasoning but he tried to develop his own philosophy of freedom in the spirit of Mill's essay. Of course he went beyond Mill's limitations in this respect as we have already pointed out. Perelman especially went beyond the simple description of liberty as "protection against the tyranny of political rulers." The New Rhetoric regards Mill's definition as the precondition of all social freedoms but does not limit itself to this negative description. Freedom also has a positive meaning which should be explored more deeply than its negative aspects. It is above all our ability to determine the pattern of our life. Perelman quotes an entire pleiade of modern European authors of various persuasions to substantiate this concept. He refers

---

[1] Chaim Perelman, *The New Rhetoric and the Humanities*. D. Reidel Publishing Company, Dordrecht Holland/Boston, USA., p. 138, 1979; John Stuart Mill *"On Liberty,"* chapter 1, in *The Philosophy of John Stuart Mill*, ed. Marshall Cohen, New York 1961, pp. 187–188.

to Littre, the French lexicographer, who wrote that authority is what authorizes, whereas power is what enables. Therefore, there are elements of morality in authority which do not necessarily exist in power. (*Ibid.*, p. 238) According to the English bishop, Butler (18th century), power is connected with domination whereas authority is based on moral superiority.

According to Jacques Maritain, power exercised without authority is in the hands of gangsters and tyrants. It seems that Maritain, one of the greatest contemporary Catholic political thinkers, continues the line of St. Augustine, according to whom supreme power not controlled by justice is nothing more than *summa lactrocinia* (*robbery enthroned*).

The influence of Saints Augustine and Thomas Aquinas is seen even more distinctly in the statements of Maritain that every power lacking authority is unjust and the separation of power from authority is like the separation of force from justice.

Perelman continues that terminological and philosophical tradition. He writes that authority always has normative aspects and that power without authority forces an individual into "submission but not respect," (*Ibid.*, pp. 139–144).

The New Rhetoric therefore is regarded by him as an instrument which can only be used by democratically constituted powers responsible for the progressive and humane direction of an organized political community, because force cannot and should not be the effective and sole motive for obedience.

> To exercise power it is essential that it be recognized as legitimate and that it enjoy an authority that brings about the consent of those who are subject to it. This is the necessary role of ideologies. Whether they are religious, philosophical, or traditional, they aspire, beyond truth, to the legitimacy of power. (*Ibid.*, p. 143).

We have already discussed ideology and its meaning. Perelman's considerations tend to express a very important and indeed a very democratic idea. Every power should seek to act like an authority and to be regarded as an *authority*. This means that it should enjoy respect, but respect does not come by itself, it must be won. Various ideologies, be they religious or secular, tend to legitimize an existing power. These ideologies however, can exercise that influence only when the people appreciate and observe their tenets, or at least, start to adhere to them. The role of the New Rhetoric is to gain or increase the adherence of minds to the arguments of the speaker and therefore it can exercise an important influence on politics and democratic evolution.

The New Rhetoric is meant not only as a simple tool of any power, but as an instrument of democratic power. It cannot serve as a means to gain adherence to mindless authoritarianism because tyranny or despotism is first of all based on physical power. Of course it has to appeal to the public, but it is able to do so only on a basis of intimidation, gaining uncritical adherence to publicly proclaimed platitudes and meaningless slogans.

That is not a genuine voluntary adherence, but an outward acquiescence by popular institutions and people.

This clarification of Perelman's theory of power, authority, and ideology is necessary not only for its own sake, but also because in his various writings there are differing definitions of the word ideology. He uses this word in different ways. For instance, in the same essay on "Authority, Ideology and Violence" (published for the first time in 1969 and then in 1970, in Brussels) he writes, in connection with naturalistic or positivistic philosophies, that every

> value judgment conceals an interest, the rationalization of desire. Every ideology is only the false mask for schemes in behalf of the strongest. It is in the works of Marx and Nietzsche that this thesis is clearly brought forth (*Ibid.*, p. 143)

It is clear that in the above sentences, Perelman uses the word ideology in various meanings, although in my opinion he remains faithful to his general conclusion that an effective ideology must more or less truly reflect political activity.

No wonder, therefore, that Perelman regards a philosophical critique of the dominant ideology as a forerunner of revolutionary action to overthrow the existing political order. A philosophical critique of such an ideology reveals the "sophisms" which are used to legitimize existing authority and power, he writes. When does a true revolution start? Perelman's answer:

> As soon as power is considered as the simple expression of a relationship of forces; a revolutionary force serving antagonistic interests can immediately be opposed to it (*Ibid.*, p. 143)

This observation by Perelman can be regarded as a general view of revolutionary change. An existing power can be stable only so long as it commands authority, as it is respected and believed to be acting for the benefit of the whole nation. The moment this perception fades, power is conceived as nothing more than sheer force (*blosse Macht*) not deserving respect and as a consequence it cannot and will not endure. It also means that revolutionaries who want to change the status quo must present their ideas as a plan for a better order, more humane and more just.

> They must, in addition, defend new order which will be more just and humane, which will save man from all kinds of alienation and give him back his lost freedom. A new ideology will have to be created to show the superiority of the new order over the established order (*Ibid.*, p. 143)

Here we also have a further elaboration of the theory of revolution. The old order which the people want to reject along with its dominant ideology must be presented as inferior to the new order, which should be perceived as superior thanks to the fact that it will be more humane and will save the people from existing forms of alienation. Consequently, it will proclaim an ideology which provides more respect for individual dignity, more personal freedoms, and democracy (*Ibid.*, pp. 143–144).

Here we see the political role of the New Rhetoric. It is an instrument to help elaborate a new ideology more compatible with human dignity and freedom which therefore can and should gain and increase the adherence of the majority of those who seek more democracy, freedom, justice, and equality. It is, however, imperative that adherence to the old ideology should diminish, whereas adherence to the new ideology must be acquired and increased. This is the cycle of social and political development and it does not matter whether various stages of this development are called revolutions or reforms. Human oppression and degradation must be perceived not by others, but especially by the oppressed individuals themselves; their understanding can be helped by explanations about how misled they had been by the obsolete dominant ideology and how necessary it is to change their life and to embrace new ideas.

The relatively peaceful demise of communism in Eastern Europe is the best example of this type of social and ideological development.

The public felt alienated from their governments and from the work they were engaged in. According to the dominant communist ideology they were told they were the "subjects" or authors of history but they found that in fact they had been pawns manipulated by cynics. Eventually, the political and intellectual oppression, economic privation, and ideological deception came to be widely understood and it became clear to them that it would be disastrous and downright pernicious for them to go on as they had. The struggle against various forms of alienation and oppression became powerful. Slogans soon became a new ideology that promised a better life and more freedom. The bankruptcy of the communist system was economic, political, moral, ideological, and philosophical. All these elements should be regarded and interpreted as a single entity. The construction of a new life without combining both material and spiritual elements cannot be successful; the hazards on the new road to reconstruction are very numerous.

It seems that until the present (1993) many social groups in the former Soviet Union have not yet fully assimilated how utterly the system of thinking and governing, initiated by the November revolution, in 1917 had failed. It may be that the inertia of ideological conservatism is even more powerful at this stage than the dire economic plight of the country. It was nevertheless inevitable that the new ruling elite in time discovered that they were unable to rule using the old methods. It is also significant that many members of the old elite began to think seriously about retiring many years ago. The Poles, Czechs, Hungarians, Germans, and the communists of other nations understood this horror before it was too late and therefore the recent, truly revolutionary, transformations were relatively peaceful in those countries. Wherever the communist rulers refused to give up their powers voluntarily, violence and bloodshed have surely followed.

Ten years earlier Perelman wrote the following general remarks which today constitute a good philosophical commentary on the European events we have been witnessing.

I conclude therefore, that if social and political life are not to become a pure balance of forces, we must recognize the existence of a legitimate Power whose authority rest upon a recognized ideology. A critique of this ideology can only be made by another ideology and it is this conflict of ideologies that is at the base of our contemporary spiritual life. To deny conflict among ideologies is to foster dogmatism and orthodoxy and allow political power to dominate the life of thought. Denying all value to ideologies is to return political life to an armed struggle for power from which the most influential military leader will undoubtedly emerge successful (*Ibid.*, pp. 144–145)

After the fall of communism this caveat should be directed to the parliamentary democracies. They can themselves endanger their own existence.

CHAPTER V

The Course of Argumentation

1. UNDERSTANDING THE DISCUSSANT

Our first purposes in process of discourse should be to establish: a) the essential ideas of the interlocutor; b) to discover his real purposes. Could the other party to the dialogue possibly fail precisely to express his/her ideas or purposes? Why are they murky, cloudy, or inadequately enunciated?

If we are aware that our partner is confused, we should seek the reasons and endeavor to understand his stance more clearly and distinctly, possibly even more clearly than he himself is able to enunciate his ideas.

We should also consider that ideas sometimes fail to agree with beliefs held by those expressing them. There may even be a flat contradiction between them. In any event, when such a discrepancy exists there almost certainly will be divergence between the ideas expressed and real purposes.

Ideology does not always represent an inverted picture of reality, as Marx asserted. Rather, it covers some aspects of reality, either enhancing some of its elements or distorting them. As a matter of fact it falls short of reality. In other words, ideology does not always represent the actual social reality either from the conservative, or the progressive, or even revolutionary point of view. Ideology operates with half truths. This does not mean, however, that one's intention is deliberately to deceive. More often than not one is the victim of one's own conviction and the first object of one's own intellectual and manipulative bias.

When we enter into a discussion with someone who expresses seemingly detached ideas that appear to be illogical and philosophically incoherent, we should establish the real ideological sense and grounds underlying the person's words. It sounds paradoxical. We should discover the person's ideology, the gist of his beliefs and interests which he himself may not clearly understand. We should know him better than he knows himself.

It is especially important to be able to assess whether the ideas (ideology) of our interlocutor are on the conservative or the progressive side.

Are they innovative, reformist, or are they a part of an ideological tradition? And, most important, is he in favor of democratic freedoms and free elections: we should evaluate them primarily from the viewpoint of the prevailing political tendency and atmosphere.

2. INNATE POWER OF CONSERVATISM

The general political atmosphere, and especially the prevailing conservatism, powerfully influence individuals, the press, and other mass-media. Thus they influence the tactics and ways of argumentation.

The editor-in-chief of the *Washington Post*, Benjamin C. Bradlee, for instance, made a great reputation out of publishing courageous reports on the Watergate scandal. Some years later, however, under the Reagan administration, his journalism became less aggressive, as he himself admitted. This means that the *Washington Post*'s presentation of political events tended more toward conformism. Why? Benjamin C. Bradlee explained: "Subconsciously the press was worried about its liberal image, and somewhere along the line people said: 'Well, we'll show him that the liberals can get along with the conservatives.' And in fact, we did have better relations a little bit with the Reagan White House than we had with Carter's."[1]

This sincere admission demonstrates the mechanism of political influence on the press and mass media better than any scholarly studies and analyses could.

Why did people worry so much about their liberalism under Reagan but disregarded it under Ford and Nixon, not to mention Carter, who after all represented a very conservative trend in the Democratic Party? The most convincing answer perhaps would be to state that the journalists had been less constrained under Nixon; he could be "kicked around" (his own expression) due to his own image and the fact that his dirty tricks ("tricky Dicky") were so well known. No one could dare to deny his involvement in immoral political foul play. Reagan, on the other hand, was able to identify himself with the entire conservative governmental establishment and at the same time with the interests of the people. The press, therefore, as the voice of the people, did not want to be perceived as antagonistic to the prevailing conservative political and social structure. The power of the conservative establishment is usually so great that it exercises a far reaching ideological influence by its mere existence. In the course of dialogue one should consider all the imponderable circumstances which might indirectly influence the perception and impact of one's argumentation.

The orator should always keep in mind that conservatism, by its very nature, is more powerful than innovative ideas; that the most powerful argument in favor of the conservatives is the mere fact that what they defend is what exists. They are therefore in a privileged position because they do not have to prove

[1] *The New York Times*, National, June 22, 1981, in: An Editor Who Left his Mark in the Capital, by David E. Rosenbaum, p. 6.

anything. They do not have to justify their position because the public usually tacitly accepts Hegel's principle: what exists must be reasonable.

The motto of Descartes, on the other hand, *"Cogito, ergo sum,"* (I think, therefore I am), translated into the language of political conservatism would be a pleonasm: I am, therefore, I exist, and therefore, I should be. Whoever questions this conservative *ultima ratio*, the highest and ultimate wisdom, has to fight against tradition, reality, and those eternal values that are regarded as real because they have been accepted in the past.

Why are these values indisputable, eternal and real? If you ask this question the answer is the simplest one: Because they exist.

The New Rhetoric is an instrument for shattering the foundations of a defective reality and its image. It is an indispensable tool for a struggle against the *status quo* of traditional injustice and prejudice.

3. ARGUMENTATION IS NOT BARGAINING: THE PROBLEM OF "CENTRISM"

The purpose of the rhetorical dialogue and the argumentative process is not to find "a middle ground", or to "split the differences". The purpose of dialogue is, if possible, to gain the adherence of the entire audience to our arguments, or at least, to gain followers for our justified and well-presented cause.

Rhetorical dialogue is not a process of bargaining; it is not based on the famous Roman principle *do ut des* (I give so that you reciprocate).

In politics as well as in business a compromise is frequently sought and reached. A compromise may often be advisable and reasonable. A decision to accept a practical compromise on the basis of bargaining may be a good policy. After that, from the rhetorical viewpoint, one should keep one's powder dry, always preparing new and convincing arguments to improve the given compromise in the direction we seek.

For the sake of illustration let us analyze the political tactics employed by President Gorbachev in 1990 and 1991. In the Fall of 1990 he inclined toward the "new Soviet Right," the Communist old and new conservatives, the hard liners and dogmatists, who wanted to preserve the new political and social achievements with the more traditional political and economic system, with the Soviet type of federation and the "leading role" of the Party in its traditional way.

The adherents of reformism, progressivism, and "revisionism" wanted quicker changes toward a free market economy, the expansion of democratic liberties, and their legal guarantees, the reorganization of the Soviet federation and new initiatives in establishing a peaceful foreign policy.

When Gorbachev moved toward the progressive camp at the beginning of his tenure, he was welcomed in America and all over the western world as an indispensable pillar of the "new world order" (as proclaimed after the "cold war"). Whenever he hesitated or played ball in the court of the conservative dogmatists, the west condemned him and even questioned his reformist credentials.

On July 1, 1991, *U.S. News and World Report* observed:

> So far, the Soviet president has not shown that he is ready, willing, or able to dismantle the communist system that produced him – or that he can survive the challenges from the reformers and reactionaries alike. Rival politicians, many of them more committed than Gorbachev to dismantling the discredited old system, are springing up in the cities and the republics. Gorbachev himself, meanwhile, continues to act as if the *"center" is the solution rather than the problem* (italics by M. Maneli; p. 39).

The correct rhetorical reasoning is this: the "center" can sometimes be a "solution" but sooner of later it can sometimes inevitably, become a part of the question, if not the essence of the entire problem. One more remark, in general, is appropriate here: whenever we speak about the "center" we must ask the basic question, from what viewpoint is the "center" the center? What elements, factors and dimensions should we take into account in judging? What interests have been sacrificed and which have been preserved?

The same reasoning applies to the American political "mainstream." This expression is especially important at election time when both parties accuse the other of deviation from the "mainstream." The ideological terminology, which can be politically attractive, can be vicious – if it is not rhetorically explained; it should not be narrowly or "precisely" defined, but analyzed in all its aspects, appearances, and innuendos. The "centrist" or "mainstream" position can be useful and reasonable, but its reasonableness must be proved not only on the basis of transitory convenience, pragmatic temporary benefits, or linguistic convenience.

4. WHAT DOES IT MEAN TO GAIN THE ADHERENCE OF AN AUDIENCE

The purpose of argumentation is not simply that one should drop one's previous view and accept the speaker's. Such a purpose would be too narrow, too simplistic and abstract. That might be the aim of a "formal logician", "mathematician," or even of a dogmatist (be he theologian or secular ideologue). From the viewpoint of practical activity and social pluralism, however, as understood by the New Rhetoric, the purpose of dialogue is to gain the *Adherence* (italics, M.M.) of the audience in order to pursue our practical ends.

Professor Carrol C. Arnold, in his introduction to the American edition of Chaim Perelman's *The Realm of Rhetoric* (University of Notre Dame Press, Notre Dame, Inc. 1982), clearly and precisely presented that question:

> In discussing that aspect of every arguer's *rhetorical* situation Perelman makes a happy choice of terms. Instead of writing of "acceptance" and

"rejection" of claims, he speaks of the arguer as seeking "to elicit or increase the adherence of an audience" (*"provoquer ou accroitre d'adhérence d'un auditoire"*). The *adherence* reminds us better than such terms as "accept-reject," or "approve-disapprove" that a *choice* rather than an *irrevocable commitment* is all we can hope for in arguing. We can only engage with someone else or with ourselves for the purpose of eliciting degrees of adherence or allegiance to ideas. This is the work of rhetoric, not of formal proof, and it is the nature of all argumentation (p. vii).

Perelman's concept is the result of his humanistic approach which is compatible with general humanist theory concerning the question of persuasion and exchange of ideas. Once we agree that people are neither robots nor machines, we must draw consistent consequences from the fact that they are thinking individuals who have acquired many ideas and convictions that are different if not inimical to those set forth by the arguer. Furthermore, they may be living in circumstances that condition their present convictions and discipline them to change their minds. The arguments of the speaker therefore can appeal to their reason, but they may harbor many emotional reasons for their resistance to new views. Perelman's precise term therefore is that the arguer has already achieved his purpose, at least partially, when he is able to "elicit or increase the adherence of an audience." In other words, the audience is not required to change its philosophy, ideology, religion, or any other deeply felt opinion formally or officially, but the audience should decide to cooperate with the speaker in the near foreseeable future in order to achieve certain strictly defined common aims. This is the meaning of "eliciting" or "increasing" the *adherence* of the audience.

This part of Perelman's reasoning also shows that the New Rhetoric is not an abstract theory, but that it is a philosophy of practical activity enlightened by consciousness and reasonableness.

In order to achieve such an "adherence" of the public one should take into account not only the general "spirit" or "attitude" of the given nation, society, or any other limited audience, but also the complicated, mixed, and even contradictory feelings of an audience.

One of the great masters who understood and was able to play on the mixed emotions and reasonings of the American public was Lyndon B. Johnson, the experienced, shrewd, politician who ultimately was elected the vice president, later on the president of the United States. Indeed, he himself, as a personality and politician reflected the antagonisms of his epoch and nation.

Robert Dallek, biographer of Lyndon Johnson, quotes the comment made by Charles de Gaulle, the President of France, when he came to the United States in 1963 for John F. Kennedy's funeral: "This man Kennedy, was the country's mask. But this man, Johnson, is the country's real face" (Robert Dallek, Lone Star Rising, Lyndon and his Times, 1908–1960 in *Newsweek* July 22, 1991, p. 52).

DeGaulle's remark reflects one of the basic ideas of the New Rhetoric concerning the connection between society, politics, national polings, and political leaders. There is always a certain link between the political culture and the morality of a society on the one hand, and the intellectual level and moral attitudes of its political leaders on the other.

Charles de Gaulle wanted to express that the Americans are less sophisticated and humane, but more brutal in social and political matters than Kennedy had officially pretended. Americans were unprepared to pay for internal idealism and expensive foreign policy. They were too realistic and too "materialistic" to pay for adventurism. Lyndon Johnson, according to de Gaulle, appealed more than anybody else to the public's "common sense," prejudices, and feelings. He appealed to those who were blaming those unable to help themselves, combining egoism with compassion and *sui generis* generosity.

On the other hand, Johnson's personality did not reflect the image painted by his other biographer, Robert Caro: "He displayed not only a genius for discerning a path to power but an utter ruthlessness in destroying obstacles in that path, and a seemingly bottomless capacity for deceit, deception and betrayal" (*Newsweek*, p. 53 – 7/22/91).

Robert Dallek, in contradiction to Caro's opinion, stresses that Johnson, indeed, combined two personalities and embraced many ideologies at the same time.

He was an ally of the Southern democrats for two decades, but in 1957 he pushed through the first Civil Rights legislation.

Dallek refers to Johnson as the mouthpiece of a big business, of oil and gas barons of his native Texas, but on the other hand he protected the program of the New Deal and continued to do so even when that policy had ceased to be fashionable. He violated campaign laws, pirated Senate elections, inflated his war record, connived for the sake of conniving. He even acquired his ranch in an underhanded way. Yet, as an elected official he worked harder than anyone else, he demanded a lot, he used to take much from the people, but he gave much in return. Dallek believes that only a few politicians had deeper concerns for the national well-being. Johnson's proverbial skullduggery can fill a dozen of biographies, but at the same time he had "genuine and extraordinary compassion for the disadvantaged – not simply when it became politically convenient in the late fifties and early sixties, but dating from the thirties when he drove himself day and night to help Blacks, Hispanics, and poor white Texans and secretly aided Jewish refugees from the Nazis to enter the United States" (*Newsweek*, 7/22/91, p. 53).

The upshot is that Lyndon Johnson drove himself and those around him unsparingly. It was a Herculean chore to compile a list of his accomplishments; he was a genius serving his own ends and the greater good of all at once.

If it is true that Johnson was not a "mask" of the nation but a true representative of the American people, then his personality is a reflection of the complicated nature of this nation: good and evil, at the same time; egoistic and altruistic, cruel and compassionate, inclined to isolationism but wanting to take responsibility for humanity's affairs.

It may be that this image of Johnson and America is either too simplistic or too complicated, but from the point of view of rhetorical political theory there should be no doubt that the great leaders of any nation are created by events in the image of their own people, their actual traits and desires. They can adjust to the lowest instincts and they know how to lead in order to achieve higher goals.

Without the type of knowledge, understanding, and ability as represented by Lyndon Johnson, it would be difficult for any speaker to produce arguments which would "elicit or increase the adherence" of the people to support desired controversial political ends.

5. UNCLEAR POLITICAL IDEAS: THE QUESTION OF SOVEREIGNTY

At a time now when the prevailing, more or less traditional ideologies, secular or religious, have demonstrated their bankruptcy, humanity has also become confused over political, legal, and philosophical terminology. Let us limit ourselves to juridico-political terms.

One of the basic concepts in political and juridical sciences is "sovereignty". It is most important in analyzing this question to ask: should we distinguish between the sovereignty of a state, of a nation, or of a government? Are those concepts identical? If not, what are the differences and what are the consequences of the distinction?

Is it reasonably possible for a state to be absolutely sovereign and independent at a time when the interdependence between states and nations is so closely knit? Is this interdependence not growing and penetrating ever more deeply into society and even individual life?

On scholarly reflection, would it be admissible to distinguish sovereignty in the legal sense as opposed to political and economic sovereignty?

Mortimer B. Zuckerman, editor-in-chief of *U.S. News and World Report*, in his editorial of June 3, 1991 (No. 21) wrote:

> More recently, Japanese investment in America has come to symbolize an increasing loss of control over our economic destiny. An astonishing 73 percent of Americans say they fear Japan will eventually own most of America – even though total British investment in the United States remains higher than Japan's.

Is not the "loss of control over our economic destiny" a partial limitation upon our state sovereignty? Or is it perhaps only a limitation upon national sovereignty or sovereignty in the sphere of economics?

Why do Americans fear that today it is sovereignty ("control over our . . . destiny") which is at stake? Mortimer B. Zuckerman speculates:

Japan is perceived as a mighty machine. . . . What has heightened these perceptions is the sheer speed at which Japan has emerged as an economic, technological and financial power. In less than two decades, Americans have seen Japanese products dominate many traditional American markets – from autos to modern airplanes – and Japanese technological capabilities surge past America in many of the industries of the future (*Ibid.*)

Thus an additional question emerges to further complicate the already confused ideas of sovereignty: is the loss of sovereignty a process or a clearly defined "condition," an "act," or a stubborn "fact?" The answer that there are various stages or degrees of "increasing" or "decreasing" sovereignty is not sufficient because the problem of what sovereignty is has only shifted to the area of murky verbs and particles which explain even less than nouns do.

There is another problem connected with these quotations: is the question of sovereignty entirely objective or is it to a certain degree also subjective, determined by perceptions? Once upon a time a famous British statesman observed that the only way to make the international situation worse is to say that it is becoming worse. Can this half-ironic and half-philosophical remark be applied to sovereignty?

The editors of *Politics and Morality* (No. 1, 1991) analyzed the information that had come from a number of sources to the effect that the decision to stop the fighting in the Gulf early, without having overthrown the dictator Saddam Hussein, was caused by the Saudi Arabian government. That is what the Saudis demanded in order to preserve a "Sunni" government. The American government headed by President George Bush thought they could not refuse. Why?

Was the American government not strong enough in these mutual relations? The answer could be: we depend on oil imports; we do not want the sheikhs to withdraw their deposits from American banks; we want to secure their market for our exports (especially weapons). It seems that the reasoning was: in order not to jeopardize these interests, it was better therefore to accept their various political demands concerning the preservation of the Sunni government in Iraq, and their Saudi's wish that the U.S. tolerate their legally remaining in a state of war with Israel and the consequent economic and political boycott against that country.

If all the reasons for American inferiority in dealing with the Arabs in truth exist, then subjection to them would be a political and economic necessity. There is nothing one could do about such partial loss of sovereignty. From the rhetorical point of view, however, we must question whether the facts are really facts and whether the perception of them is correct. Perhaps we should take into account other possible facts such as the possibility of importing oil from other countries, developing new sources of energy, or finding other markets? Lastly, the international and domestic resentment over the fact that the bloody, terroristic, inhuman Iraqi dictator and his equally bloody and ugly regime and party have remained in power is a factor that should be included in the moral and political assessment of the political and military options.

If the second alternative is more reasonable and should have been chosen, then a limitation on American sovereignty was not caused by objective factors, but by subjective political ideas and economic interests. The question of sovereignty, full or limited, therefore, also becomes subjective and not purely objective because the assessment must be the result of rhetorical analysis.

The very competent and careful *New York Times* columnist, Flora Lewis, observed that (the administration)

> has ceded to Saudi Arabia an influence on American policy that blocks the pursuit of American purpose. . . . The U.S. went along with the Saudi view that it is better to leave Saddam Hussein in power than risk a rebellion that might destroy the Baath regime. . . . That is why Shiites and Kurds were left to be massacred, and Mr. Hussein was allowed to retain his still impressive forces. . . . The U.S. accept Saudi judgments on Gulf politics as gospel, and virtually identify American interests with Saudi interests. (*The New York Times*, July 19, 1991, p. A-27)

Why does this happen? Flora Lewis' answer is very simple: "As an oilman President Bush sees their point."

The same idea is expressed and elaborated in the book of Bob Woodward, *The Commanders*. It describes the activity of the Saudi Arabian ambassador, Bandar bin Sultan, a relative of King Fahd. He gained direct access to the White House and to members of the cabinet. He used all available diplomatic tricks to push the U.S. into the war and ultimately did his best to sell the Americans the self-serving Saudi proposal wrapped in an ideological package which could be accepted by the American Congress and public.

The Saudi interests are elemental: they want to preserve the *status quo*. Therefore the Bush administration invented the word "stability"; they created a new political sacred cow. Whoever is against the despotic rulers of Saudi Arabia and Kuwait is against "stability" and is allegedly also against American interests. The Saudis are less interested in the problem of the Shiite's fundamentalism than they are afraid of democratic tendencies in the Gulf region. It seems that the State Department and the closest advisors of the American president either do not understand it or do not want to accept such an evident fact. If Americans however are following a policy so strongly advocated by absolutist and dogmatic ally, if the responsible politicians do not accept the obvious fact that "Saudi concerns are different and must not obsess U.S. policy" (*Ibid.*, Flora Lewis) then the sovereignty of the American people and its government is being undermined.

From the theoretical point of view, however, one can ask a very basic question: how is it possible that a superpower, a bastion of democracy in the world, can compromise its independence and constitutional freedoms by acceding to such foreign pressures?

The discussions about the relationship of the American and Saudi governments demonstrate how difficult and murky the problem of political sovereignty is, particularly due to oil, banking and other economic interests, and how important rhetorical argumentation is to analyze such questions in all their aspects. One should start the analysis with the concept of sovereignty which is a typical political "unclear idea" and go through as many elements as possible determining the existence of the status which cannot be defined precisely. The fact that the assessments concerning sovereignty are determined by objective and subjective factors adds confusion to any solution. Additional rhetorical observation concerning the problem of sovereignty is that one should not be afraid of words and express the alleged heresy: the sovereignty of the U.S. Government in its dealings with certain foreign governments and power centers is curtailed, because of economic and political interests, because of objective and psychological reasons, and because of certain vested interests and privileges, which are perceived to be especially important.

6. UNCLEAR IDEAS: "TO CUT THROUGH ABSTRACTIONS"

From Dupréel, his teacher and friend, Perelman developed the concept that unclear ideas can contribute to the improvement of societies. We analyzed the idea that a "centrist" position in politics may be a problem rather than a solution. On the other hand, a "centrist" position can be an unclear and confused idea, but still can represent a workable plan or scheme. There are many social situations when a truly successful method of proceeding cannot be developed, either because of objective difficulties or because of the resistance of those who do not believe in the new plan or refuse to support it, no matter how clear and objectively beneficial the plan may be. They prefer to persist in their "centrist" unclear ideology, than venture to enter unknown areas.

"Centrists" consequently often become objects of public ridicule and even contempt.

A popular Soviet comedian often poked fun at Gorbachev's "centrism." One day he declared and Muscovites used to repeat: "to left-wingers, he's on the right. To right-wingers, he is on the left. He sees himself in the center – but that's an optical illusion."

From the rhetorical perspective it should be asked: how do we know that the position even of an unclear "optical illusion" is relatively better or worse than plainly wrong ideology? The "illusory" centrist position may be the one that affords more time to make more enlightened and reasonable decisions later. Once we give up dogma we lack an eternally perfect criterion or ideal against which we may measure policies.

In the critical years of 1990–1991, Gorbachev was unable to decide how to save the Soviet economy. Should he make radical changes favoring a "free market" or should he seek to preserve and reform gradually (if possible) the old system of "socialism" and super-centralization?

The Soviet economist, Grigory A. Yavlinsky, compiled a far-reaching plan with a group of experts from Harvard University. The project was decisively rejected by the dogmatic, incorrigible, right-wingers of the USSR who had prepared their own plan. Gorbachev announced a compromise to try to combine the two plans.

"Grigory A. Yavlinsky . . . tried to convince Mr. Gorbachev that in economics, as compared to politics, there can be no compromise, no marriage of "left" and "right," no "third way" between the past and the future" (*The New York Times*, June 29, 1991).

It may be that Yavlinsky and the Harvard experts were correct in their assumption that the best way to save and develop the Soviet economy was the plan they had put forward. Nevertheless, from the viewpoint of rhetorical methodology, they committed two basic errors.

Firstly, let us suppose that what is possible in politics may be impossible in economics, maybe that is an "absolute" truth. However, these two spheres are so closely interconnected and so interdependent that nearly any important economic decision becomes a political decision, and vice versa.

Secondly, the development of liberal capitalism to the monopolistic stage and into a "welfare state" is an indication that a "third way," as the Catholic Church and the West European socialists preach, is indeed possible. It may not be the most successful way, but it worked for many decades; do we have any better proposals?

The dogmatic statement, therefore, that "compromise" or a "third way" in economics is impossible should be regarded a dogmatic, unreasonable, assertion. In the transition from super-centralization to a free market economy, various "intermediate" stages must be bound, various compromises made which may appear to be superfluous to an outsider, if not impossible or contradictory in themselves. Indeed, they may be necessary in order to overcome social inertia and to gradually increase the adherence of the nation to the new ideas, institutions, and new way of life.

The New Rhetoric, in principle, agrees with Hegel's observation: history must repeat itself twice; the first setback of progressive evolution will be followed by a second movement in order to persuade the people that the advent of new times is inevitable and they should no longer regret that the previous phase has come to an end. Consequently, after every revolution, a new kind of restoration follows which at any rate is not a return to the *status quo ante* but does prepare a new assault on "the unreasonable reality," as Hegel wrote. Those who observe this course of events from the rhetorical viewpoint should, however, not remain passive, indifferent onlookers. At every stage of the struggle, actions and counteractions, they should analyze, persuade, and promote activities which serve freedom, human dignity, tolerance, and the rule of just laws. We should establish which partial reforms and even small adjustments better serve our ideas of justice and freedom in any situation and avoid those which increase suffering and enslavement.

This is the rhetorical view of compromise and of political "centrism" which also serve as foundations for rhetorical outlook on humanism.

The New Rhetoric is neither a theory nor a methodology envisaging a new paradise, but it does promote the slow process of creating a new reality. The famous U.S. Supreme Court Justice, Thurgood Marshall, used to refer to it as "another world out there."

After justice Marshall's resignation from the Supreme Court, Professor Kathleen M. Sullivan remarked:

> As Justice Marshall retires, we may read his eloquent admonitions in dissent as prophecies for another (perhaps distant) era when the political pendulum swings again. What marked those dissents was a candor that cut through legal abstractions to the social reality and human sufferings underneath (Kathleen M. Sullivan, "Marshall, the Great Dissenter," *The New York Times*, June 29, 1991)

The philosophical and social sense of the New Rhetoric is encapsulated in those words honoring one of the world's greatest humanistic jurist: "to cut through . . . abstractions to the social reality and human sufferings underneath" (*Ibid.*).

7. GENERAL AND CONCRETE IDEAS

It has become almost an incontestable truth, a truism accepted by democrats, that without more active social participation in the political process the democratic system will be weakened and could decline. There will inevitably be many political and economic theories and ideologies which for various reasons appeal to people. The main criterion for determining whether a democratic system is functioning normally and efficiently is the conscious participation of the public in the process of making political decisions; they should reasonably adhere to certain ideas and make up their minds after a reasonable assessment of alternatives. When citizens analyze their choices deeply, when they reach reasonable conclusions, democracy and society profit. When they consciously prefer one policy and support it critically, they should nevertheless remain open-minded enough to change their adherence whenever they find that the situation and circumstances have changed.

The democratic process is an endless dialogue and the public should know about it and understand it. Otherwise, they may become the victims of clever demagogues.

The New Rhetoric is an achievement which may be instrumental in any field of practical activity, whenever we depend on "practical reason."[2]

---

[2] Professor Harold Zyskind wrote that the New Rhetoric is a notably important achieve-

The term "practical activity," or simply "practice," has been used deliberately. Human practice is always inseparably connected with the process of
thinking that demands choices and the overcoming of obstacles. These are
not the result of pure thought, but of life and activity. The New Rhetoric had
never been intended as a mere philosophical or methodological system, but
as an instrument promoting reasonable activity, practice, enlightened by
reason.

We emphasize practice, but we find that we must also invoke basic or
universal values.

Two criteria of the universality of values (principles) may be considered,
according to Perelman. We can all invoke certain universal values like truth,
justice, beauty, etc. (*Justice, Law, and Argument*, p. 68). And we can invoke
less general values, principles, or norms which have the advantage "of not
having to be justified – not because they are self-evident, but simply because
they are not contested" (*Ibid.*, p. 68).

General agreement can be reached on such general norms as for instance:
one should do good and avoid evil. No one should be made to suffer unnec-
essarily. We should always aim for the greatest good of the greatest number.
The principle of conduct must always be valid as a rule of universal legislation (see *Justice, Law, and Argument*, p. 66).

Unfortunately, general agreement on the validity of these general rules
does not mean that all the participants in a dialogue should agree on what is
good or evil, just or unjust in a given situation in which different people
have various ideas about their personal and social interests.

As Perelman wrote: " . . . Our agreement lasts only so long as we remain
on the level of generalities. As soon as we try to pass from this agreement *in abstracts* to some concrete applications, controversy begins" (*Ibid.*,
p. 66).

This is the second basic social and intellectual rule which is the point of
departure for the founder of the New Rhetoric: the "innate," "natural," unavoidable, contradictions exist between universally known, appreciated, and accepted
general values and principles and their more *concrete* understanding, interpretation, and application to life.

It is obvious that different applications are caused by social, economic,
and political differences; philosophical contradictions are unavoidable in any
society. Abstract thinking which is so unique and specific for humanity is
incontrovertibly pregnant with contradictions which must be clarified in the
course of discussion.

The principles of the New Rhetoric and as art of discussing, arguing, and
persuading should be known to every intelligent and educated person in the
modern industrial world in which warfare and the use of naked force are

---

ment in philosophy, logic, ethics, etc., and "generally any field which depends on practical
reason", (italics, M.M.) Harold Zyskind, "Introduction to Chaim Perelman's *The New Rhetoric
and the Humanities, op cit.*, p. ix.

morally unacceptable. This is an instrument – whatever name we give it – that should be used by civilized nations and people in order to preserve peace, mutual understanding, and tranquility.

8. NEW DILEMMA OF CAIN

The famous answer of Cain in the Bible that he was not his brother's keeper and his subsequent punishment by God stimulated Judeo-Christian theologians to proclaim the moral principle that we are our brother's keepers, that we should help our brothers to avoid evil and to choose good.

Needless to say, this maxim was too general to be carried into practical effect without controversy regarding its meaning and practical content. It seemed to put too many and too demanding obligations on individuals. Such a heavy burden cannot normally be undertaken.

The situation has changed dramatically since 1950's, however. The changes in human, political, and international relations with their increase in mutual interdependence, have created a basis to reconsider Cain's dilemma. The traditional liberal and libertarian point of view of the limited obligation of an individual toward his neighbor and society has been important in the evolution of our culture, including our notion of privacy.

It must, however, be reconsidered and reassessed. The well-being and even the life of nations and humanity as a whole can depend on certain activities (or omissions) by small groups, even individuals. Human errors, for instance, caused and contributed to the horrendous disaster of Chernobyl, USSR. Consequently, a new precept is developing: we should pay more attention to the interests and actions of our neighbors and observe their and our behavior in a situation which might be harmful for many people. One must assume the unrewarding role of being "my brother's keeper," helping him or imposing restrictions on him against his will.

There is a new type of activity which can be regarded neither entirely nor clearly illegal. We have to employ new terminology, there are activities "semi-illegal," or "would-be-illegal," because of the new provisions of international law and the new norms of morality, many of them slowly gain public support and acknowledgement. For instance: The United Nations Convention on the protection of the environment prohibits any action which could endanger the life, health, and well being of humanity caused by destruction of the environment. How should these new legal norms be interpreted or applied?

During the Gulf-War of 1990–1991, the Iraqi government decided to set fire to hundreds of Kuwait's oil wells and to release millions of barrels of oil into the waters of the Gulf.

According to the latest interpretations of law and morality, these actions were both immoral and illegal and the perpetrators should be punished.

The events described here are a drastic example of a new, very broad problem. It is so new that for the time being we lack the precise legal and philosophical rules to apply to them.

Destruction of the global environment harms the life of all humanity and every individual. If we are serious in the belief that one should apply the basic common law principle and wisdom that whoever inflicts harm should make amends (the same in Code Napoleon), then we should insist that those who destroy our environment must make good the damage. It does not matter whether the destroyer has acted deliberately or recklessly – he should be held responsible for his actions which have harmed humanity. It is possible that reckless environmental destruction will cause the death of many people, from cancer, respiratory diseases, brain damage, etc.

This is the great rhetorical, legal, and moral philosophical problem which should determine responsibility for such actions, omissions, mindlessness, or simple indifference.

We know that the destruction of the ozone layer can be the source of numerous catastrophes and diseases. We also know that dumping various substances in the ocean can slowly convert the ocean into reservoirs of sludge and poison.

We know that the dumping of waste into the Rhine and Oder rivers in Germany and Poland by certain nations has caused terrible consequences for contiguous nations.

Are we not obligated, in this situation, to rethink the Biblical admonition concerning being our brothers' keepers? Can we allow modern Cains to act as if they were the sole proprietors of the world? Do they have a truly unlimited right to claim that their homes are their castles? Should we not impose new obligations and restrictions? Do certain interpretations of the Bible, modern Humanism and New Rhetoric meet by accident?

We are slowly entering a period when the control by the more enlightened people over the morally backward has become a necessity.

Even more complicated and potentially disruptive is the influence of military technology on the political situation. Let us put it bluntly: modern weapons, be they nuclear or chemical or bacteriological, in the hands of irresponsible dictators create clear and present dangers to the life and even the existence of nations, continents, and in fact, the entire globe. Both superpowers and now the successors of the Soviet Union had atomic weapons. They have been able to control their use and opinion has even been voiced that the fear of mutual destruction has preserved the peace. Nevertheless, we dare not take a chance that criminal autocrats and dictators, in desperation, will refrain from seeking to impose their will or take vengeance by using weapons of mass destruction.

Today we know that democratic governments question the use of such weapons, and tend to be more responsible whereas autocratic governments are usually completely irresponsible.

The extermination of entire groups of people and even of entire small nations and tribes has been carried out by dictatorial governments such as in Cambodia,

Nigeria, Syria. Previously this pack was led by Nazi Germany and Stalinist Russia.

These considerations lead to a non-traditional but logical conclusion: we all are interested in securing democratic governments in every country of the world. Our concern should not be regarded as an attempt to interfere in the internal affairs of a nation but as an act of self-defense by individual nations and by all humanity.

From this point of view one can assess the behavior of the allies when they permitted Saddam Hussein to continue his criminal activity. The president of the United States, George Bush, argued that we had no right to interfere in the internal affairs of Iraq. This question should be reversed. Do we have the right to permit Saddam Hussein to continue to exterminate the Kurds, Shiites, and other innocent people? Do we have the right to allow Hussein to continue his efforts to produce atomic weapons or other weapons of mass destruction? Do we have the right to believe a professional murderer and liar whose guilt has been proven beyond a reasonable doubt? Do we have the right to risk the life of all his neighbors and perhaps even entire continents? Does the American president have the right at the advice of this Saudi allies to expose the American public to the blackmail of such a dictator when he finally will acquire weapons of mass destructions?

All these considerations lead us to conclude that we have to rethink and re-evaluate all our experience, legal norms, political principles, and moral rules. One can at the same time argue, however, that Kant's Imperatives, Judeo-Christian and traditional Humanistic precepts of morality are still valid, provided they are reinterpreted and applied in a reasonable and creative way to the new demands and the new situations. When you love your neighbor, you should help him to be free from the threat of irresponsible dictatorships. Today we know exactly which regime or government is more or less democratic and responsible, and which is totally cruel and anti-human.

In order to achieve the role of saving nations and humanity from disaster we must apply new methods of thinking and discussion, a completely new method of argumentation and persuasion; we cannot leave even one stone of traditional beliefs unturned – this is philosophy and methodology of the New Rhetoric.

CHAPTER VI

Politics, Law, and Morality – A New Phase

1. NEW MORAL MAXIMS

At this time, a substantial change in the relationship between politics, law (domestic and international), and morality is underway. Let us concentrate on three basic phenomena:

1. There is growing cynicism in the world concerning the relationship between politics and morality. The public, more than ever, is convinced that this link has been broken because politicians seem to care less and less about moral standards.

Indeed, apart from the private morality of the actors on the political scene, moral considerations and the need for an appearance of morality are increasingly more influential although politicians themselves have not become more decent or moral themselves.

2. People think that questions of morality cannot be discussed in a truly scholarly way, that they are beyond the realm of reason, that moral norms must be arbitrary, based on a *priori* system of values. But, in fact, thanks to the influence of rhetorical argumentation and developments in the sphere of law and legal interpretation and application, contemporary moral norms are more concrete so that they can be elaborated rationally and substantiated.

3. Since 1950's, we have entered a phase in which certain moral, humanistic, and humanitarian principles have become well entrenched in domestic constitutional as well as international law defending human dignity and fundamental human rights. Although these were the result of the evolution of our morality, the situation recently has changed so radically that they now constitute new and generally accepted criteria of morality.

The Geneva Conventions of the XIX–XX centuries, laid down a series of humanitarian laws. They created norms for peaceful solutions of conflicts and the administration of international justice. They prepared the ground for a completely new phase in the mutual relationship between politics, internal and international law, and morality. The ensuing outbursts of international legislative activity after World War II, the decisions of international courts trying war criminals, the Charter of the United Nations, and innumerable

64

conventions, declarations, and all kinds of normative documents adopted by the United Nations, as well as new concepts of legal and moral philosophy, created a new phase in the relationship between politics and morality. Never in history was this interdependence so close or so important, although the "man in the street" seems to be more cynical than ever and one is rather convinced that these two spheres are so far from one another that only a foolishly naive person would believe otherwise.

A close analysis of these questions contradicts this popular "street" wisdom. There has been, as we shall try to demonstrate, such a deep change in this respect that even the famous opinion of Albert Einstein that after the invention of the atom bomb everything changed except human thinking, is questionable.

When we assert that there are new connections and associations between politics, law and morality, we refer both to objective and subjective changes, their mutual objective conditioning and their reflection in philosophical perceptions.

2. TWO SPHERES OF POLITICS AND MORALITY

While assessing the problems of politics and morality we must distinguish two dimensions.

One is the great question of political orientation and the fundamental direction of economic and social development. Those are issues which determine the life or death of nations, if not of humanity. They can drastically influence the health and general welfare of this generation as well as of future generations.

The second dimension represents the day-to-day, political struggles for influence, for position and honors, for greater income and privileges, for a seat in parliament, in government, the town council, leadership in clubs, political parties, churches, etc. This is the area of intrigues, lies, half-truths, false advertisement, exaggeration, underestimation. Briefly, mudslinging, charges of deception, calumny, false promises, and pious lies.

Here the basic rules of the political game remain the same, as they were described many centuries ago in Thucidydes's *Peloponnesian War*, in Machiavelli's *Prince*, in Bacon's essays, and in Shakespeare's plays. According to them politics is a jungle and in it, as they all demonstrated, one must act according to the rules of war in endless competition, like it or not. In the political struggle good intentions do not count; political success is all that does. The victors are not condemned when they are shown to have been involved in normal little lies and misdemeanors, sometimes they get absolution for big lies and grave transgressions. Success absolves many sins. Today, however, everything is more complicated, because there is a direct link between the second and the first type of politics in relation to morality.

Today, Machiavelli's *Prince* and *The Discourses on the First Ten Book of*

Titus Livius need not be interpreted primitively and applied as the art of deception to secure immediate political ends. Any political success, however limited in time or space, is nevertheless a step toward obtaining and securing future gains. Therefore, one is able to prove against appearances that not "everything goes" today; what is considered immoral can be more harmful politically than ever before. In our times these two levels of politics are so closely interwined that sometimes they are inseparable.

We all remember the words the King pronounced in Hamlet, "Madness in great ones must not go unwatched" (Act III). It is a problem, however, to determine who is and who is not great today. Which problems are great, which are unimportant. That is the question! Whatever the answer, one thing is sure, the course of events has imposed new requirements on the morality of political decisions.

* * *

Today, anyone who studies the problem of the relationship between politics and morality will agree that the subjective will of the given politicians notwithstanding, they are required to reach decisions compatible with the broadly understood requirements of morality. The need for at least the appearance of morality in political behavior in this epoch of mass media, TV, radio, and the press, becomes increasingly more cogent. Politicians have to take into account the need and power of such appearances because otherwise they will fail. Machiavelli's old advice that it is more important to enjoy the reputation of being honest, religious, and loyal than actually to be so, has acquired a new meaning. We have many convincing examples on the American political scene to support this thesis.

It is generally accepted that the fall of President Richard Nixon was caused by his moral rather than his political and legal transgressions. From the juridical point of view he was not proven guilty, but the moral atmosphere surrounding the Watergate affair had become unbearable so that in a short time he became an ineffective lame-duck president notwithstanding his landslide reelection (1972).

The unethical behavior of ex-Senators Tower and Wright in the 1980's, shows how dangerously vulnerable they had become. They had to leave the political scene although not so long before then they had been powerful and very influential.

The 1991 scandal surrounding the private air trips of President Bush's Chief of Staff, John Sununu, shows that the public was hardly upset about the relatively small sums involved but felt morally insulted. The disregard for elementary modesty and decency infuriated people. The president therefore, with great reluctance, had to limit Sununu's freedom to use military aircraft for personal travel and finally Sununu had to leave the White House.

There is a similarity between the abuse of power by John Sununu and the former Communist East German party boss who had headed the Communist trade unions for fourteen years. The German court, chaired by chief judge, Hans-Juergen Herdemerten, did not strictly consider political or even financial charges against him, although it did find that the diversion of 57 million in union pension funds to the organization of Communist youth might arouse "suspicion of manipulation." In June 1991, the court decided that the use by Mr. Harry Tisch of $46,000 for the vacation of himself and Guenther Mittag (Communist chief economic boss) was an illegal abuse of power. It sentenced him to eighteen months in jail.

As he announced the verdict, the chief judge addressed the question that the sentence was relatively light, according to public opinion. Many might have felt disappointed. The judge explained to "the people of Eastern Germany" that the court "could not fulfill political expectations."

The analogy between the abuse of power by Sununu and Tisch is striking. It could happen in an atmosphere of bureaucratic arrogance, an "arrogance of power," as Senator Fulbright used to call it, of moral and legal irresponsibility on the part of bosses who regard public institutions and funds as their own feudal fiefdoms and property. But then the social and political atmosphere and moral sensitivities in both countries were different.

Americans still regard their state and government as their own and basically approve of its activity, whereas the Germans regarded the East German regime as foreign and imposed upon them; it was a despotism and a tyranny and its political leaders were looked upon as outlaws who had seized power without legitimacy. It was a regime of *magna latrocinia*, as St. Augustine wrote.

Consequently, the fall of the East German government in 1989 was also the fall of Tisch. His "normal behavior" was then deemed criminal; whereas the abuses of power by Sununu were perceived as "normal," and "non-criminal," although "politically improper" and "morally wrong" (some jurists nevertheless argue that his transgressions were illegal as well). Sununu was not punished, he was not even formally dismissed and there were no public protests or outcries against him or against the President for retaining him. This shows that American society has become "morally numb," that the traditional "protestant ethic" has eroded and deteriorated more than expected. George Bush and his advisors did not share the illusions of many religious or humanistic moralists; they depended on the public's numbness.

The upshot of all this is that due to political and moral perceptions in a given society Harry Tisch was sentenced to jail, whereas John Sununu who spent much more of public funds for personal pleasure and recreation enjoyed the good graces of the President for a long time and he is politically active.

3. OLD PRINCIPLES – NEW INTERPRETATIONS

Achievements in medical technology have made so called surrogate mothers possible. It would seem that from the political, juridical, and social points of view there is nothing wrong in a contract for childbearing between a married couple and a would-be surrogate mother. Commercial principles, the provisions of contract law, agreement and especially *do ut des*, compensation with consideration so highly prized in free market societies, have been strictly observed. The only misgivings, however, are moral, and they prove overwhelming. France's Supreme Court (Court of Cassation) endorsed the argument of the solicitor general that "the human body may not be lent out, may not be rented out, may not be sold" (1991).

In this way, the contrary opinion of the Paris Court of Appeals was reversed. The Paris Court, in its decision supporting surrogate motherhood stated that it is an expression of free will and individual responsibility for those who do it without any concern for profit.

The French solicitor general argued that one cannot accept the point of view of certain states of the United States of America which regulate and legalize such contracts and address only the additional juridical aspects of surrogate motherhood because – and here is the second moral argument – it could lead to a situation that one could start choosing the mother according to the color of her eyes, her hair, etc., and one could thus plan the human race.

Let us observe once more that the arguments of the French court and the solicitor general that one should not plan the human race or treat the human body as merchandise, are moral and philosophical arguments. It would indeed be very difficult to find any justification for this point of view in any provisions of law in any contemporary state. The contrary may in fact prove to be true: certain totalitarian regimes have tried to improve the human race. Eugenics has a long tradition beginning perhaps with Plato and ending, for the time being, with Nazi Germany.

Once public opinion, including that of jurists and politicians, regard such an issue as one pertaining to human dignity and the inviolability of the human body which must remain *extra commertium*, the whole problem becomes primarily moral. Thus it was the prevailing morality that determined political and juridical decisions in the sphere of new human relations technology.

* * *

Let us analyze one recent example to consider the question of the influence of moral feelings in the sphere of international law and politics. We know how enthusiastic Americans were immediately following the victory in Iraq in 1991. Several weeks later, however, the euphoria subsided and, according to polls, the majority questioned whether a victory had actually been won or only a public relations triumph. Why? Because Saddam Hussein had not only not been removed but he continued to massacre Kurds, Shiites, and other political "infidels." Hussein's continued genocide and the default of western powers to protect helpless people caused moral revulsion. The reputation of all participating governments was tarnished when the murderer's actions remained unpunished and the perpetrator escaped scot-free. A.M. Rosenthal, the columnist for *The New York Times*, wrote: "In Iraq it was failure of moral stamina and political compass by a president and a few of the men around him," (*The New York Times*, June 1991).

Such is the essence of the new relationship between politics and morality: the failure of *moral stamina* leads to political detriment if not downfall. When actions do not accord with the requirements of morality, international as well as domestic, condemnation follows. This maxim is gradually growing into a golden rule in political relationships and morality; its observation is necessary for success in politics.

Do we need any better or more convincing proof that questions of morality can be analyzed rationally, that we are able to reach reasoned, justifiable conclusions? That is what the *humanistic* and *rhetorical* theory of morality is all about.

* * *

One of the reasons that certain philosophers and logicians say that moral norms must be arbitrary and that there cannot be any scientifically grounded moral principles or reasonable directives of moral behavior, is that it is a nature of moral norms that they are very general.

The situation has changed in recent decades and we will analyze the new phenomenon using rhetorical argumentation. Today, when we discuss the questions of politics and morality, we must start from the basics once more, from the very meaning of what morality is and what politics is.

The traditional view of morality as the norms determining what is good or bad, what behavior, activities, or postures are right or wrong, raise questions of political decisions and attitudes, of law and its observance, violation, or deliberate rejection.

One can object to all the traditional definitions of morality, that they actually define idem per idem what is unforgivable either in formal logic or in Aristotelian/Perelman rhetorical argumentation.

We must finally break away from moralistic generalities to find other ways of defining what is moral or immoral. We should take into account progress in philosophy and in modern humanism. We must reconsider previous social experience as well as current manifestations, the trials and tests of modern states and legislation, including free market, western welfare governments, and eastern socialist states.

Moral norms and maxims have remained general and imprecise for many centuries. In the Judaeo-Christian world, both believers and non-believers were prepared to accept the fact that certain Biblical commandments could be adhered to as a basis for morality apart from any agreement about whether the Bible was divine or human. People have become accustomed to the Golden Rule as a guiding rule: do to your neighbor what you would have him do to you. This maxim can be expressed in many other ways, both positively and negatively.

The Kantian imperatives, both the Categorical and Practical, form a very specific version of the Golden Rule: always act in such a way that you can at the same time wish that your actions become a universal law. In other words, one should act as if one were the legislator for the whole world while respecting the humanity of one's neighbor.

The moral requirement of Communist morality, as expressed in the most simplistic Soviet and Chinese writings, can be narrowed down to the principle that whatever supports the interest of the proletariat, its struggle for social liberation, construction of the classless society, and victory of the revolution all over the world, is moral.

The practice throughout the centuries has proved that all general maxims can be interpreted in various contradictory ways; they frequently serve as a tool for persecution and extermination, as a justification for terror. General norms of morality, religious and secular, may lead to either humanistic idealism or the most vicious inhumanity.

It would be unrealistic to suppose that moralists, philosophers, and theologians will be able to reach a uniform, non-contradictory view of what is moral or immoral, just or unjust, good or evil.

On the other hand, however, practical human activity, social experience, and especially new developments in domestic and international law have become decisively helpful. Practice frequently overcomes theoretical differences.

On the basis of the new provisions of international and domestic laws accepted all over the world, on the basis of primary constitutional principles, and lastly, on the basis of the activities of public, governmental, social, and political associations and institutions, we can regard activities and norms which are instrumental in achieving the following objectives as moral:

a) maximum happiness of individual, with protection of life and the health of societies first of all;

b) protection of individual privacy, of freedom and tolerance;

c) protection of human rights as defined by the whole corpus of the international documents, especially those of the United Nations;

d) active fight against international criminals and crimes against humanity, as defined by the respective documents of the United Nations and regional organizations.

The basic modern principles of our morality, as elaborated here, do not prejudge questions of general moral theory and its sources, whether they are secular or divine, juridico-positivistic, or emanating from "natural law." These principles of morality should be considered to be the result of the development of the whole course of our civilizations in the west, of our philosophy and jurisprudence, activity of governments, of municipal legislators and international law. From the viewpoint of historical experience and the rhetorical theory of argumentation, the cycle of recent developments in the sphere of politics and morality can briefly be presented as follows: the recognition of moral norms and sensitivities leads to new domestic and international legislation. After the general acceptance of the new juridical norms that protect human rights and liberties, they become a new code of political morality. They form a set of more precise, better codified, criteria for moral evaluation.

The earlier evolution of moral sensitivities and new moral requirements of life paved the way for international and constitutional norms that guarantee democratic freedoms, human rights, protection of the weak, restrictions on the excessive prerogatives of governments, which – while practicing genocide – hide themselves behind the wall of sovereignty. A more precise, better codified set of norms has evolved to serve as criteria for moral evaluation.

The moral conviction that the wall of sovereignty cannot and should not be regarded a Chinese wall within which the rulers are absolutely free to commit crimes has been developing for a long time. It is only recently, however, that these feelings have been transformed into better elaborated and more precise norms on international law.

* * *

In May, 1991, the majority of the United States Supreme Court judges ruled, five to four, that physicians and nurses working in family planning clinics which are federally subsidized, will no longer be permitted to mention abortions to pregnant women, even women who had been raped or were victims of incest. Abortion as an option to terminate pregnancy shall no longer be discussed, recommended, or referred to. The patient must be denied this essential medical information.

According to many critics, this decision shows that the five justices who ruled on this problem violated the provisions of the First Amendment to the Constitution which stipulates that "Congress shall make no law . . . abridging the freedom of speech or of the press." Any physician, therefore, should be able to enjoy the unabridged freedom to tell or advise his patients how to correct or ameliorate their medical condition. The decision of the court could also be deemed immoral since it is every physician's moral duty to present to his patient the full extent of the status of his/her health.

An atmosphere of confidence also should prevail between doctor and patient as otherwise certain therapeutic measures could prove ineffective.

Even the mere possibility of a patient's suspecting that a physician is insincere or morally compromised as a mere mouthpiece of authorities, creates a situation that could be deemed immoral, a transgression of the Hippocratic Oath, detrimental to the mental and physical well-being of the patient.

This example demonstrates that neglecting the moral aspects of a professional relationship, will lead to attitudes and decisions inimical to constitutional principles concerning freedom and human dignity.

Furthermore, this example confirms our basic thesis that disregard for moral norms leads to a situation that is "unconstitutional" per se; both partners of the dialogue are intimidated, consequently insincere; they say one thing but mean another.

And, vice versa: the interpretation of constitutional and other legal provisions in a despotic, totalitarian, spirit by justices who tend toward increased authoritarianism, leads to a course of moral distress, consequently, immorality in social and private relations.

4. THE PROBLEM OF GOOD INTENTIONS

One of the basic Greek and Judeo-Christian concepts of morality must be revised: good subjective intentions – or Kantian good will – are not sufficient criteria of morality. The defense of war criminals, for instance, that they acted on orders or in good faith, is not acceptable by itself. On the other hand, a rebellion against oppression may today be justified not only morally but juridically. Domestic and international law have elaborated an entire catalog of binding do's and don't's.

Whether "moral stamina" or intentions must necessarily be subjective features of a given politician or personality, or whether they may simply be connected with a well rounded political shrewdness, is another matter which does not pertain to these considerations.

There is no reason for us to investigate what the intimate, personal feelings and persuasions of individual Polish Roman Catholic bishops and cardinals may have been who, as a Church body, an Episcopate, signed the famous pastoral letter (1991) condemning anti-Semitism and the sins of omission on the part of those Polish Catholics who failed to help their Jewish compatriots during the Holocaust when they could have done so. The letter leads to an important conclusion: one may be held responsible for genocide not only by commission, but also by omission.

In this way, the present generation of Polish Catholics contributed greatly to the theory of the relationship between politics and morality. Whatever the sources of the inspiration may have been, "divine," "Catholic," "secular," or "humanistic," the results will be far-reaching.

The idea that the crime of genocide may by committed by omission – so competently elaborated by the Polish Episcopate and by Father Stanislaw Musial, S.J., – is a brand new moral and theological concept. The definition of a crime by omission, in case of genocide, should be generally applicable to the spheres of morality, jurisprudence, and international relations (see: M. Maneli, "Anti-Semitism and Moral Responsibility" *Freedom Review*, No 4, July–August, 1991).

This is indeed one of the most profound and far-reaching changes in the relationship between morals, politics, and jurisprudence.

Slowly, the entire political picture of the modern world will evolve toward new moral responsibilities.

There is no doubt but that the American and European nonfeasance of

exposing the Kurds and other Iraqi nationals threatened by Saddam Hussein
to mortal danger, will be considered especially grave when viewed and interpreted in the light of the new theory espoused by the Rev. Stanislaw Musial,
S.J., and the Polish Bishops. The "failure of moral stamina" may indeed be
unforgivable. The Kurds and Shiites have been decimated; genocide has taken
place although it could have been (easily) prevented. The decision not to
intervene was immoral, illegal, and ultimately politically mistaken.

This is the gist of the evolution in our century; new requirements of morality,
legal consciousness, and social conscience became the source of new international and domestic legislation, which afterwards became a new criterion
of morality for assessing political activity and decisions.

Thus, the moral norms became less general and ambiguous, more precise,
more to the point, more concrete and easier to apply.

5. STRANGE MORAL PRAGMATISM

The above was the title of an interview with Jacek Kuron, one of the leading
intellectuals of Poland and Europe who has been able to combine various
careers as a politician, author, ideologue, organizer of illegal activity under
Communism, political prisoner and lastly, a brilliant statesman who has been
involved in governmental functions since the downfall of the totalitarian
regime. He has been a senator, minister, and one of the leaders of the new
democratic opposition to the democratic government of Lech Walesa, and once
more an ideologue.

In the interview quoted below, he demonstrated that he had learned the
rhetorical way of thinking and arguing in the field of politics and morality
without having had any special training. This interview illustrates once more
that today the rhetorical way of thinking may coincide with common sense;
it results from experience and pragmatism combined with reasonableness and
moral responsibility.

Reasoning and rationalism, as presented by Jacek Kuron, constitute a
meaningful example of Rhetorical Argumentation and a thoughtful contribution to the analysis of the convoluted relationship between politics and morality.

Jacek Kuron began his anti-Communist and anti-totalitarian activity during
his student years at the end of the 1950's. After the "Polish October" of
1956, he befriended Adam Michnik and Karol Modzelewski, other young,
intellectual and political leaders. During the ensuing thirty years or more
they became leading intellectual political champions of the anti-Communist
opposition; they founded KOR, the Committee for the Defence of the Workers.

Michnik and Kuron spent many years in Communist jails. Immediately after
their release, they participated in the famous Round Table conference, sitting
not far from their former jailor, the Minister of Security, Czeslaw Kiszczak.
Michnik became the editor-in-chief of the important daily of *Solidarity* and
Kuron advanced to become Minister of Social Affairs in the first post-

communist government in 1989. When the new president of Poland, Lech Walesa, split the *Solidarity* movement and changed the government, Michnik and Kuron once more returned to the opposition. This time a democratic opposition against a democratic government.

In July 1991, Kuron was interviewed by *Polityka*, one of the most serious weekly newspapers in Poland and in Europe. The occasion for the interview was that Kuron had publicly expressed displeasure with an article published six weeks earlier by his friend, Adam Michnik. The interviewer, Janina Paradowska, formulated her question in the following way:

> Michnik-Kuron, Kuron-Michnik. An inseparable duo. They say that even Professor Geremek[1] was confused as to who was who. And you say that there are quarrels between you?

Kuron replied:

> My friendship with Adam began in 1958 and was based on the fact that we would have disputes. It was good for us because as a result of these disputes we reached what was richer, wiser, and made more sense. So these disputes have lasted until today. There was a period when it was inadvisable to bring these quarrels to light and at times those who did not know us well and by chance witnessed our disagreement were astounded. . . . You should realize, Madam, that the essence of disputes is that *both sides are right or at least that they are partially right* (italics – M.M.). Therefore, friendship, without disputes, is poor. Truthfully, I even doubt that such a friendship is possible.

The interviewer asked Kuron about his reaction to Michnik's statement that in today's Poland there is less and less space for those who prefer moral principles over political advantage. Why does Kuron disagree with Michnik's view that there is only a limited possibility for participation in current politics by people who are relatively older and disinclined to make any compromises with their consciences (Michnik obviously had referred to people like himself who preferred to go to jail rather than compromise their ideals with the Communist regime). Kuron's answer to this question is significant:

> I understand Adam's moral uneasiness which always accompanies participation in politics and is now especially appropriate. I reject this simple contradistinction between ethics on the one hand and politics on the other. It is harmful for many reasons. It is not true. It is the popular conviction that participation in politics must be amoral.
>
> It is not so. Moral conflicts take place in politics frequently, as they do in everyday life. It is illusory to believe that one can live without moral conflicts. . . . The prejudice which I mentioned is the result of what took place in the Party Committees which is extremely harmful for our

---

[1]   One of the leading intellectuals of *Solidarity*.

democracy, indeed, for every democracy, but especially dangerous in Poland because such a small percentage is politically active. . . . There are, of course, situations in which we can be politically engaged without moral conflicts. That happens, when we simply give testimony. In the old times when we protested that someone had been arrested, that the government used anti-Semitism or violated the Constitution, then we simply gave testimony to the truth. Indeed, we had no moral conflicts then. But even in this period there were those among us who argued that we were immoral because we attracted young men to our activity who later were punished for it by being kicked out of the university or their jobs.

The interviewer then asked Kuron about the morality of his activity when he became a Minister in the government of Mazowiecki. His answer was:

Our luxurious situation from the ethical point of view, has changed. . . . We had to make decisions during the upheaval of the masses. . . . As a Minister I had to decide whom to give more money, whom less? At times these decisions led to a person's poverty, perhaps even caused deaths in a hospital because money was not available. Anyone saying that this activity was not connected with tremendous moral conflict simply does not know life.

I fear that you, Madam, are helping to popularize another prejudice, that there are two types of people, those who work for higher ends, who sacrifice themselves for others and those who struggle for personal ends. In fact, most people including politicians, take various values into account in their lives. One may work very hard, consistently, daily, because one fulfills one's own personality; in this work and in this way one reaches one's personal ambitions. I can only work. I have done nothing in my life except what I wanted to do, whatever was my passion. I could not do otherwise. It is unimportant whether I do it as a Minister or as the president of a foundation which I established, myself. What is important is both what I am doing and how much of my heart I put into it. Therefore, when I was appointed Minister and later dismissed, nothing changed.

The interviewer then asked: what about those who prefer to withdraw from politics? What do you say about them? Kuron's answer was:

That means that others should make the decisions? This is an immoral attitude, in my opinion. This is an escape from responsibility. I can understand that someone is tired, no longer has the strength, and is withdrawing. I accept such a solution. But please, do not confuse it with morality.

Kuron later argued that all decisions in life and politics should be made taking into account lesser evils. When the situation is more difficult, the responsibility is heavier.

Therefore, if he had a dispute with Adam Michnik in Switzerland, their discussion would have been strictly academic. It is not so in Poland in the

1990's when one has to participate in politics in order to decide the question of how to solve the problems of chaos, democracy, and authoritarianism. One must act and act purposefully and efficiently. There is a danger of chaos in Poland, Kuron stressed. Democracy contributes to this chaos. On the other hand, it would be impossible to preserve democracy and develop it using authoritarian methods which some politicians recommend:

> It may be a paradox that if you want to develop democracy the means which are in accord with our values are the most efficient. I confess that this is a very *strange moral pragmatism* (italics – M.M.). Of course, in the short run, one can deceive the public with slogans, but such a policy will soon be punished with a vengeance. It is better to tell the people that the democratic reconstruction will take years, that it will be difficult, but in the final accounting, our efforts will be rewarded. . . . I do not believe that an efficient dictatorship is possible in Poland. Such a concept and prospect is immoral and inefficient.

The gist of Kuron's ideas can be reduced to the following:
- true, personal and/or political friendship and cooperation must be based on dialogue, pluralism, and an exchange of thoughts which, in the course of argumentation, reach deeper and become wiser and richer;
- one should actively participate in political struggles, because otherwise one becomes neither purer nor more worthy by inaction. We usually resolve moral dilemmas for many reasons and in various ways, at times, even sub-consciously;
- it is frequently easier to make a moral decision during a fight against a clearly defined enemy or when acting in the underground, say, against an invading army or a totalitarian party of autocratic government. We have no such moral "comfort" or "luxury" under more normal circumstances, especially in a transitional period on the way toward democracy, and in democracy itself;
- to make decisions in the public interest such as decisions on allocating resources is to make choices; such choices can hardly ever be detached from morality.

The conclusion is: since it is impossible to escape from political and moral dilemmas, one should use the power of thought and argumentation to resolve them as humanely and rationally as we can. The New Rhetoric serves to improve understanding of the choices.

CHAPTER VII

Sociological Laws

1. NEW RHETORIC AND MODERN NOMINALISM AND REALISM

The New Rhetoric has bridged the artificial chasms that were created by philosophies at the end of the nineteenth century. Two influential German intellectual centers, especially those in Freiburg and in Marburg (represented by Rickert, Windelband, Cohen, Natorp, Cassirer) argued that there are two types of sciences: the natural and the socio-historical. The natural sciences, according to them, discover natural laws, generalize empirical facts by seeking and finding uniformities. The scientists aim to predict future events and prepare humanity to act efficiently according to the predictions.

The historical sciences, however, according to the schools which have neo-Kantianism as their foundation, cannot draw generalizations from historical, social, or political events. They are interested only in concrete particular events which can never be duplicated. Historical events, according to them, therefore are unpredictable. Furthermore, they claim that history only teaches us that we are able to develop our intelligence and acquire a great deal of knowledge but that we cannot learn anything from it that might have concrete, practical value in making decisions involving new problems in new circumstances. Paradoxically, there is only one lesson that history teaches us: it is that there are no lessons.

Perelman, aside from Marxists and theologians, was the most serious philosopher to have rejected the sharp dogmatic contradistinction between the natural (nomothetic) and the historical and social sciences: "Nevertheless, we don't have to draw unjustified conclusions from this distinction that the historical sciences are concerned with everything that is concrete and individual in opposition to the nomothetic sciences which study abstract laws. In fact, every science is obligated to set limits and consequently to neglect certain aspects of reality. The criteria of selection are however, clearly differentiated" (Chaim Perelman, *The New Rhetoric and the Humanities*, Dordrecht, Holland: D. Reidel Publishing Company, 1979, p. 146).

The New Rhetoric, first of all, takes into account a very simple and generally admitted fact that both types of sciences must study "repeatable phenomena." Both have to find similar structures and regularities which allow us to "consider them as patterns of a type of phenomenon" (*Ibid.*, p. 146).

Historians, unlike natural scientists, are not interested in objective, static reality; they seek generalities in the course of events. They limit their investigation to those elements, happenings, or aspects which, according to their scale of values, merit being regarded *significant*, which are *worthy* of being considered *historical* facts because they are convinced that future politicians, social activists, and philosophers will learn something by knowing them.

Here, however, historians find difficulties which natural scientists overcome more easily. Historians (politicians, ideologues, etc.) can and must disagree on what is significant, important, meaningful, indicative, and valid, and therefore deserves our attention. Social scientists may even quarrel as to what constitutes a fact and what is only an appearance. For instance, from the day of the cease-fire of the Gulf War, 1991, there have been disputes as to whether the US and the allies had really won the war or whether what was called a victory was an illusion, because Saddam Hussein had retained his power. What does being victorious mean? Diverse interpretations have been given about the result of the hostilities.

The rhetorical principle that we do not invent great personalities but that we help to form their images, is also applicable to events that are described as significant. We explain a person by his acts, we explain events by links of co-existence and links of succession (Perelman, *The New Rhetoric and the Humanities*, pp. 147; 150; 151). Even if we claim that in history and society nothing exists per se, that does not mean that nothing can be observed, interpreted, or evaluated. In the natural sciences only the methods of observation and evaluation differ, but the social scientists are still able to ascribe meaning to historical events.

From the rhetorical viewpoint, the contradiction between social reality and appearance may not be absolute either. If we write a chapter of history based on an analysis of the behavior and activity of one person, as a hero who is regarded great and influential for example, we should understand that the greatness of such a person is also the result of the criteria on which our judgments are based, that we either admire or disown certain appearances while the reality was simultaneously "generally formed from other appearances" (*Ibid.*, p. 150). We first interpret then decide what events and persons are significant.

The endless disputes over historical and political categories are indeed quarrels as to whether and to what extent we are able to predict the course of events and to what extent our deliberate political activity can affect social change.

The answer to this question determines not only current practical political decisions but even more, our attitude towards political planning and social programming. All the contemporary arguments against social categories are indeed a modern incarnation of medieval nominalism. Of course we can reject the view of the "realists" who in the Middle Ages believed that general ideas were real and almost tangible. On the other hand, if we agree with the nominalists, we give up all tools for interpreting history, types and forms of societies and states. Consistent nominalists, or consistent neo-Kantians could even be in trouble defining democracy and autocracy, defining what reforms are and what revolution is. To argue that only concrete specific phenomena can be described, means that there can be no general conclusions at all. It also precludes enlightened decisions concerning our individual and social behavior, our present situation and our political future. Even worse, one cannot accurately describe past phenomena because their historical context can only be expressed in general terms.

Perelman decided to use his rhetorical method against, as he writes: "The dangers of a dogmatic and intolerant realism" which seem to him "as grave as those of skeptical nominalism" (*Ibid.*, p. 157).

Historians do exactly what any intelligent person with common sense would do. They proceed from specific phenomena which took place at a certain moment and try to set forth the characteristic features of the given historical period. Every definition is, of course, as Spinoza stressed, "pernicious" because it rejects certain features and stresses others. What is regarded accidental and therefore unimportant is deleted in order to reach the essential, the most important features of the given period. This is what Perelman had in mind when he wrote:

> The Renaissance was not only the rebirth of classical letters, it was the birth of a new man, a new vision of one world, a new way of being in the whole, therefore the renaissance of letters was only a limited event within the total transformation of society. It is the same with the historian who speaks of the Age of Enlightenment, who begins with a certain cultural phenomenon, which appears among French and English thinkers . . . and makes this trait essential by designating it as such. (Perelman, *Humanities*, p. 154)

This is a good illustration of how any historical period is interpreted. The Renaissance and the Enlightenment and the subsequent rise of capitalism in Europe were periods in which innumerable new things happened. To understand them one must impose an interpretation, one must reduce to order a chaotic multiplicity of events despite the consciousness that such a proceeding inevitably distorts an unspoiled vision of the natural state of things.

At any rate without these "reductions" and "orderings" and a limited practical point of view, it would be impossible to draw conclusions concerning the state of affairs in our time or any other.

In this way we have arrived at a new problem which can be posed in the following way: once we decide to analyze the most important phenomena of the past, what measure do we use to determine what is more or what is less important? Can we argue that our current needs determine our scale of values? If our answer is simply in the affirmative we might find ourselves in the quagmire symbolized by Pokrovskij, the famous Soviet historian of the 1920's. He argued that history is nothing but current politics as applied to past events.

We know that totalitarian regimes, especially the Bolshevik and Nazi, tried to present historical events according to their political needs. They did this with a reckless disregard for facts and the truth. A similar situation exists after the cold war: there are many political parties, especially extreme rightists, who claim that their contribution was decisive in the defeat of communism in various countries. Even more farfetched is George Bush's taking credit for the fall of the Soviet regime.

Rhetorical historical analysis is also pragmatic to a certain extent, but it neither disregards individual nor the totality of events. Sometimes attempts to draw conclusions which may serve our narrow immediate interest, but it does so on the basis of an analysis of the facts which we find interesting and important. We try to draw reasonable conclusions and *submit them to the tribunal of human reason, argumentation and critique.*

When we concentrate on certain phenomena and trends, we do not do so with preconceived ideas and predetermined conclusions. Quite the contrary. Our critical assessment should be treated as stimulus to deeper studies.

The New Rhetoric can creatively interpret such ideas as Max Weber's elaboration of the *Idealtypus* (ideal type), or the *Zeitgeist*, the *Volksgeist*, the *Industrial Revolution*, and lastly, history as the *history of class struggles.* One can argue that there is something rational in every one of these general ideas but none is a full explanation of history. Writing about the concept of class struggle Perelman observed:

> History as an expression of the permanent struggle of classes gives us a new outlook, one different from national history or from the history of battles. . . . But are all these perspectives not arbitrary? Are they useful tools or do they allow a better comprehension of the past? . . . Whatever the response, we must state that categories allowing us to organize historical knowledge cannot be put aside entirely. The imperfection of the instrument which forms these categories does not result in their uselessness. (Perelman, *Humanities*, p. 155)

Let us suppose that all these categories, which we mentioned as examples and are so important to historians, will be rejected by us and set aside. We would have to replace them with others. There will simply be other historical and social categories which will be as limited and perhaps even more misleading than the previous categories.

The upshot of these considerations is that in order to understand history and in order to use historical experience to help analyze present and possible future events, one should be well-educated and versed in our cultural heritage and be open to arguments and counterarguments.

There is a saying in France that every generation of Frenchmen should rewrite the history of the French Revolution. It is of course doubtful that new generations would find important new material. Nevertheless, they will be able to interpret the same material taking into account the new world and

French experience. They will be able to create a new scale of values. Without representing a vulgar type of pragmatism, one can usually throw a new light on relationships and facts previously underestimated.

Every generation has to relive new struggles between "realists" and "nominalists." Every generation must reconsider the relationship between the essential and the accidental (*Wesentlich und zufaellig*). One can, however, agree with Perelman's general thought in this matter:

> It should be noted that the ideas of essence, of what is essential or belongs to essence, can be conceived of as the generalization of the person rising from his acts and manifestations. Also certain manifestations are considered accidental, not having to be joined to essence. The opposition between the essential and accidental is a value judgment, a judgment of importance. Those who desire to eliminate this judgment of importance from their analysis try to replace the qualities *essential* and *accidental* by quantitative determinations relative to the frequency or rarity of the qualified phenomena. But they are incapable of giving *meaning* to quantitative results without finally putting numerical data into categories which make this data intelligible. (*Ibid.*, p. 151)

It seems that the philosophical categories of essence, existence, necessity and accident, must remain in our deliberations whenever we analyze our life and future prospects.

2. RHETORICAL INTERPRETATION OF CONTRADICTIONS

Political and social contradictions were the source of the New Rhetoric, and the New Rhetoric is a means for explaining them.

The New Rhetoric maintains that social contradictions are real, inevitable, and do objectively exist. Disputes therefore also have genuine foundations and objective backgrounds.

Not only philosophers and ideologues discern contradictions within a society. The famous French-Polish movie director, Agnieszka Holland, who was interviewed in connection with her film "*Europa, Europa*," observed:

> The Epoch in which we live is a transitory period between what has ended and what will arrive. The two most important political tendencies of the twentieth century were Communism and anti-Communism. Now they have ended. In Poland and Czechoslovakia, there is a political vacuum. They introduced a free market; without a doubt it is the best form of economy, but having a free market is not a cause for which it would be worthwhile to suffer and die, and there is the danger that right-wing Fascist tendencies will fill the vacuum. (*Kurier*, New York, July 27, 1991)

One can agree with Agnieszka Holland that these two tendencies, Communism and anti-Communism, have dominated the world political scene in our century. The correct observation that they had been the dominant forces does not mean, however, that other contradictory trends were irrelevant. Sometimes in many countries other contradictory forces were more in evidence such as the rivalries between tribes, the antagonism between rich and poor, hatred between the ruling cliques and the oppressed.

On the other hand, however, many nationalistic aspirations were connected in one way or another with more basic contradictions. German, French, Italian, Polish, Hungarian and Ukrainian nationalisms, as well as many others, were so closely intertwined with anti-Communist ideology that the two were frequently identified. There has also been a famous contradiction between Clericalism and liberal anti-Clericalism. One can state, however, that anti-Clericalism had been identified by clerical ideologues as pro-Communist, whereas all liberal and socialist followers attempted to equate Clericalism with fascism and mindless anti-Communism.

After the recent collapse of the European Communist regimes it is obvious that the facade of Communism and anti-Communism was a mask that hid many contradictory tendencies and various political programs. But mankind has to pay a price for every simplification. Therefore, after the collapse of Communism and at the end of the Cold War, people are still living in a world of old demons and contradictions. They were unable to assess the new situation critically and realistically. The New Rhetoric, from its very beginning tried to persuade people that they should not take extreme positions in analyzing situations, contradictions and hostile attitudes. The general idea of the New Rhetoric is that there can be reasonable elements in any ideology.

Such a statement would have amounted to a simplification of the rhetorical attitude. What we have in mind is that, even if the beliefs of the public are completely unfounded, the reasons for their adherence to those beliefs should be explored.

Even insane attacks of political fury have their causes.

It would therefore be unreasonable to regard the eruptions of Muslim Fundamentalism in Iran as a pure anti-humane aberration. There must be social and political reasons why such aberrations and deviations from the "common sense" have become so powerful in this new age of enlightenment and the new industrial, scientific revolution. The New Rhetoric feels that no social phenomenon should be discounted as unimportant because it cannot be defended reasonably.

The rhetorical concept of audience also means that professional scholars, philosophers, ideologues, politicians or historians do not have any monopoly upon wisdom and knowledge of social laws. Therefore, we appreciate very much the observation of the film director Agnieszka Holland, that although the period of the simplistic interpretation of the contradictions between Capitalism and Communism is over, but the result is a new kind of political "vacuum."

The contradictions, according to Rhetorical thinking, do not necessarily overcome one another. They can to such as extent diminish or annihilate each other that the result is a "vacuum," a new social situation which must be assessed from the very beginning.

CHAPTER VIII

The New Rhetoric and Jurisprudence

A. POSITIVISTIC FOUNDATIONS OF LEGAL PHILOSOPHY

1. *The new rhetoric and juridical positivism*

It seems paradoxical that there is a connection between the positivist philosophy of law and the rhetorical tradition. This disbelief results from a
misinterpretation of juridical positivism and unfamiliarity with rhetoric.

The development of the New Rhetoric is the main reason why we should
take a fresh look at certain forgotten aspects of juridical positivism and its
relationship with traditional logic and rhetoric.

It is simply a prejudice to think that juridical positivism is indissolubly
bound up with formal logic. Indeed, the further development of the theory
of law in Western democracies depends partly on Western jurists' ability to
assimilate the New Rhetoric. There is a symbiosis between an updated juridical
positivism and the new theory of argumentation as elaborated by Perelman.[1]
The ground for such a synthesis had been prepared by the founders of juridical
positivism themselves and especially by Jeremy Bentham.

Legal positivism is not today's favorite philosophy. It has been held responsible for many of the vices which beset modern political regimes. In the
west, it has been re-named the philosophy of Creon. In Communist countries, on the other hand, it was accused of being a bourgeois ideology which
endangers "socialist legality." Nazism rejected it as a product of the Jewish
spirit contrary to the *Volksgeist* (spirit of the people) and the *Fuhrerprinzip*.

It would appear that all the important political and ideological forces of
this world have united to fight against legal positivism: the Thomists and
existentialists, the neo-Kantians and phenomenologists, the rationalists and the
personalists, the adherents of various natural law theories, the dogmatic
communists and revisionists, the "official" Marxists and the "opportunists,"

---

[1]   Ch. Perelman and L. Olbrechts-Tyteca, *The New Rhetoric*, (University of Notre Dame Press,
Notre Dame-London, 1971), p. 514.

the liberals and the conservatives, the spokesmen for the juntas and the African presidents, scholars in Moscow and in Washington, in Peking and at the Vatican.

What has caused such antipathy toward such formerly respectable doctrine? Political interests? Ignorance? Philosophical objections? Memories of recent crimes and abuses? Social antagonisms? All these factors taken together and separately are causes.

Let us observe that the strange amnesia seems to have overcome the most ardent critics of the doctrine; they pretend to have forgotten the important progressive role which positivist jurisprudence has played in the development of the rule of law and democracy, of social stabilization, security and individual rights.

Parliamentary liberal democracy which developed in the western world in the nineteenth century was accompanied by juridical positivism. The one has always been inseparable from the other, and they are condemned to coexist, they constitute one organism.

During the last century, democracy underwent a series of changes. One can say the same of legal positivism.

After World War II, new juridical phenomena have appeared. The war criminals who had been held responsible for the crimes committed against humanity were tried and sentenced. Almost all the nations of the world signed the Charter of the United Nations and accepted the principles of the Universal Declaration of Human Rights. Aggression, racism, and colonialism were outlawed. The principles laid down in these documents not only became part of international law, but also in various ways, of internal positive law. This development deeply affected systems of domestic law. We are dealing with new bodies of law, we face new legal systems, new positive law. Therefore, the original doctrines of legal positivism cannot continue to be rejected or supported uncritically either.

Instead of being dropped, juridical positivism must be modernized. The *aggiornamento* of many old ideas and institutions, political and juridical, is high on the agenda of our times.

The philosophy of juridical positivism never has been an uncritical "establishment" theory preoccupied with gilding and supporting the existing law and reality. But today's philosophy of juridical positivism can and should promote the creation of new legal provisions and institutions as well as interpretations and applications of existing laws. Here the New Rhetoric enters.

There is no salvation for our endangered legality and constitutional order, the preservation of our individual rights and liberties, except through the positive legal system. The theory of juridical positivism, when correctly understood, interpreted, developed, and applied, combined with the new theory of argumentation, will constitute an indispensable part of the many-sided legal order, justice and freedom. Juridical positivism received a new lease on life. And it is the New Rhetoric that can revive its heart and spirit.

2. Bentham on the nature of law and limits of sovereignty

Jeremy Bentham is generally regarded as the main founder and exponent of the philosophy of juridical positivism, and rightly so. Therefore we will concentrate first of all on the writings of Bentham in analyzing the relationship between his juridical philosophy and New Rhetoric.[2]

Like every classic thinker, Jeremy Bentham expressed at once the strongest and the weakest aspects of his philosophy and presented them in the clearest possible way. Like other classic thinkers, he has had his admirers and detractors. He is not appreciated in the twentieth century among the new ideological conservative right, and he is anathema to the radical left. Both sides have good reasons to loathe Bentham: he stood for unlimited political liberties, he criticized opulent rulers who thought only of happiness for the minority, and he spoke out for genuinely free competition.

But it was Bentham's definition of law which has become the main object of criticism. Indeed, Bentham's concept of law is inseparable from his theory of legality and his unique concept of civil disobedience. Bentham's definition of law reads as follows:

> A law may be defined as an assemblage of signs declarative of a volition conceived or adopted by the sovereign in a state, concerning the conduct to be observed in a certain case by a certain person or class of persons, who in the case in question are or are supposed to be subject of his powers.[3]

This definition concentrates on what according to Bentham is realistic: law is the will of the sovereign in a state. The legal norms separated from the entire legal corpus cannot properly be understood or observed:

> A body of laws is a vast and complicated mechanism of which no part can be fully explained without the rest. To understand the function of a balance-wheel you must take to pieces the whole code.[4]

From the assertion that law is the will of the sovereign, the accusation was drawn that positivists uncritically promoted the idea that "the law is the law," "*Ordnung ist Ordnung*" and that whoever opposed "the law" should justifiably be punished. It is a fact that this conclusion is not Bentham's, but that of his liberal and totalitarian adversaries. According to him, the people will not tolerate unlimited whims or caprices of a ruler. The sovereign may be legally

[2] This problem is discussed in detail in my book, *Juridical Positivism and Human Rights* (New York: Hippocrene Publishers, 1981). I analyzed certain elements of this question in my article, "The Traditions of American Jurisprudence and the New Rhetoric", in Etudes de Logique Juridique, vol. VII. Bruxelles, 1978 (Travaux de Centre National de Recherches de Logique. Published by Ch. Perelman).

[3] *The Collected Works of Jeremy Bentham*, ed., J. H. Burns, "Principles of Legislation and of Laws in General", ed. H. L. A. Hart (London: The Athlone Press, 1970), p. 1.

[4] Jeremy Bentham, *An Introduction to the Principles of Morals and Legislation* (London: The Athlone Press, 1970), p. 299.

unlimited, but *de facto*, his power does have bounds. Bentham gives the following example: let the sovereign attempt to prohibit the imbibing of alcoholic beverages and fornication. Will he succeed? "Not all the tortures which ingenuity could invent would encompass it . . ."[5]

Bentham warned that even the most powerful sovereign-legislator should not exceed the limits of necessity. There is no need, Bentham wrote, to limit the liberty of the subjects if there is no profit to society. If passion or prejudice inspire a legislator (as in Louis XIV's laws against the heretics) he will defeat himself and stultify his own purposes.

According to Bentham law creates duties on the one hand and rights on the other. Law does not bestow upon the master arbitrary, capricious privileges, but imposes on him a myriad of duties which he must perform (by positive or negative acts) in order to respect the *privileges, immunities*, and *exemptions* of the subjects. Corresponding to the infinitude of the "liberties" is the diversified infinitude of the duties which are admitted by the mere condition of mastership.[6]

Bentham's forgotten idea is fundamental to an understanding of legal positivism: the unlimited power of the sovereign is the source of pure slavery, and law does not apply to slaves.[7] There can be no genuinely *legal relations* between a master and his slave, or between absolutistic despotic government and its subjects. There can be no legal order in such circumstances. A country with unlimited power (mastership) would be "a spot upon the earth so wretched as to exhibit the spectacle of pure and absolutely unlimited slavery."[8] Hence positive laws must bestow not only power but also rights, privileges, immunities, and exemptions.[9] Their complexity limits the sovereign and precludes his becoming – to use modern terminology – a totalitarian dictator. The ruler is bound not by chimera of natural law, but by the greatest happiness principle and its concomitant. If the sovereign legislator violates these requirements he will sooner or later feel the consequences. Bentham even mentioned the possibility of resistance, which should not be confused with the notion of a right of resistance against oppression. Such rebellion would be principle and the very concept of true positive law.[10]

---

[5]   *Ibid.*, p. 290.

[6]   Jeremy Bentham, *op. cit.*, p. 241, ch. xvi. 42.

[7]   *Ibid.*

[8]   *Ibid.*

[9]   One element by Bentham quoted above requires further clarification: why did he write about right as a "fictitious entity?" In this respect the nominalistic limitations of Bentham's philosophical methodology and theory come to the surface. Whatever is not *corporeal*, in the strictest Baconian sense, is a fiction for Bentham, a product of the mind created for the purpose of expediency.

[10]   . . . no private family . . . could subsist twelve months under the governance of such rules (i.e. English judiciary law – M.M.) . . . were the principles from which they flow to receive their full effect, the utmost extravagance of Jacobinism would not be more surely fatal to the existence of society than the sort of dealing, which in the seats of elaborate wisdom call

The end of any law, Bentham argued, should be the greatest happiness of the whole community, of the governors and the governed together, and one should prefer the happiness of the greater number to that of the lesser number in the event of a conflict.[11] More specific ends of the all-comprehensive legislation were elaborated by Bentham in the following way: maximizing universal security; securing the existence of sufficiency and subsistence for all the members of the community; maximizing abundance; maximizing equality and inequality.

Bentham mentioned a specific principle concerning penal law: the positive pain-preventing principle. In the sphere of civil law Bentham gave various axioms concerning property. There are also many other specific ends, recommendations, and principles outlined for legislators which can be found in Bentham's voluminous writings. The above enumerated principles are relatively general, although Bentham tried to be more specific; notwithstanding his effort he never left the realm of generalities which cannot be mechanically applied even if desired. Every end, principle, maxim, or axiom needs to be interpreted and evaluated in order to be embodied into codes or practical life. And there is always the possibility that a different conclusion will be drawn from the general rule by a different interpreter. Thus an important entrance was opened for rhetorical argumentation.

3. Bentham's rhetorical reflections

How can, and should, Bentham's juridical and philosophical principles practically be applied and embodied into everyday life? He himself understood that one could draw contradictory conclusions from the same general principles:

> In each of the axioms, the antagonistic or . . . competing interests of the two parties are conjointly brought to view . . . in those which relate to subsistence, abundance, and equality, they are parties whose interests stand in competition, no blame being supposed to lie on either side. By the legislator, preference should be given to that interest to which happiness of the greatest number will be most augmented.[12]

The legislator should act as an honest broker or mediator among antagonistic groups and interests; the result can be a compromise, but each party continue to defend its own interests. In the event of competition between

---

itself by the name of justice. Jeremy Bentham. *"Rationale of Judicial Evidence"*, in The Works, vol. VI, p. 205b.

[11] Jeremy Bentham, "Pannomial Fragments" in *The Works of Jeremy Bentham*, ed., John Bowring (New York: Russel and Russel, 1962), vol. III, p. 211. Bentham did not complete this work. The last fragments are dated June 1831.

[12] Jeremy Bentham "Pannomial Fragments" in *The Works of Jeremy Bentham*, ed., John Bowring (New York: Russel and Russel, 1962), vol. III, p. 212.

interests, it is really impossible to determine who is right. Here one can sense the influence of the ancient rhetorical tradition with "no blame being supposed to lie on either side."[13]

This is one of the completely forgotten ideas of Bentham's theory of politics and morality: in case of competition and antagonisms, both sides can represent legitimate and morally justifiable interests. There is no reason to blame either for defending and promoting its own.

'If no one should be blamed for the diverse interpretations of the greatest happiness principle, that also means that many interpretations may be right.' Such a conclusion does not conform to Cartesian logic, but it is admissible from the rhetorical viewpoint. Bentham more or less consciously took a step toward a rhetorical revival. The legislator, in the final analysis, must be persuaded which solution proposed by the competing antagonistic parties is the better at any given time.[14]

In the introduction to the publication of the letters addressed to Count Toreno for the use of the Spanish Cortex (1821), Bentham drew the following rules from the principle of the greatest happiness for the greatest number required for the drafting of a new Penal Code:

- there should be many competing authors; every draft, if possible, should be the work of a single hand and the name of the author should be disclosed;
- all foreigners should be admitted to the competition with the local authors, and they should even enjoy preferential treatment;
- the test of the ruler's aptitude to rule and legislate should be his willingness to establish an all-comprehensive code.

None of his specific proposals can be regarded as inherent in the principle of the greatest happiness of the greatest number, but they reveal his "democratic," "populist" attitude and rhetorical approach.

The impact of Bentham's Introduction to the "Letters to the Conde de Toreno" lies in the fact that he himself directly connected the specific, less general, principles of legislation with his basic ethical and political principles. He went beyond logic to draw his conclusions. His conclusions are

---

[13]   In his *Essay on Logic*, Bentham analyzes Aristotelian and Socratic methods. Cf., the chapters in particular: "Aristotelian and Socratic Mode – their difference", and "The Disputative Branch of Aristotle's *Logic* – in what respects it failed", "Essay on Logic" in *The Works of Jeremy Bentham*, vol. VIII, pp. 236–238.

[14]   Bentham asked: what should be the object of any debate: Should it be to *win over* the opponent without humiliating him? "So to shape his discourse, that, on return to it, the adversary shall, for the avoidance of a still more afflictive humiliation, submit to the humiliation of coming over to his side". How could this delicate purpose be achieved? Bentham presented the Aristotelian method in his interpretation and started to explain – in contrast to this method – the Socratic method of disputation. Here the manuscript ends abruptly with the note: "Go on explaining the mechanism" – Jeremy Bentham, *Essay on Logic* in *op. cit.*, p. 238.

One can assume that Bentham wanted to elaborate on the Socratic method as being sometimes more adequate or more fruitful than certain aspects of Aristotelian logic, but he did not have a chance to return to this problem. He wrote the last parts of his *Essay on Logic* when he was already in the eighties.

reasonable – in Perelman's sense of this word – but they are not logical syllogisms. Bentham's assertion that a foreigner can be as good, if not a better, legislator in a given country than a native, is one of the most visible remnants in his writings of the eighteenth century: all people are equal, according to him, regardless of social or national origin.

Therefore, Bentham believed that he could advise any legislator anywhere in the world while living in London. At the same time, the Germans and especially the Historical School believed that it would be simply irresponsible to draft a new code before all the necessary studies had been undertaken. Codification, they asserted cannot be "elaborated," "imposed," or "legislated," must grow from the national soil and soul.

Bentham regarded that opinion as a sheer conservative, anti-democratic absurdity and he would advise anyone who was willing to listen that any nation without a code of laws or with obsolete laws should immediately begin to prepare a new code, a comprehensive one, because partial codification would not solve any problems, but rather add to the existing doubts and disputes. One should strive to reach legal certainty as soon as possible and should relinquish unnecessary excursions into the past, into the preindustrial age of darkness.

It was Bentham's opinion that the laws which existed in England and in other countries did not assure certainty because they "bristled with a certain science as repulsive as it is inexact and useless, and which owes its obscurity to its own absurdity."[15]

This is the reason it is necessary to codify the laws and to issue one code which will encompass, as Bentham recommended, all the laws, civil and penal, internal and international, political and constitutional.[16] This monumental work should, and must, be accomplished by the legislator who will be able to abolish all other legal, quasi legal, or so-called legal norms and unclear customs (mores) which have the force of law.[17] They could be removed only by the iron broom of a sovereign legislator.[18] No other alternative was available. Only the legislator, and he alone, could promulgate comprehensive collection of laws, like a *Code of Napoleon*. Bentham's recommendations constitute an important aspect of juridical positivism: it is a theory which is a reaction against complexity and uncertainty, obscurity and absurdity of laws newly introduced or inherited from previous epochs.

The legislator should forbid all attempts to introduce "unwritten" laws

---

[15]   Jeremy Bentham "General View of a Complete Code of Laws" in *The Works of Jeremy Bentham*, vol. III, p. 209.

[16]   *Ibid.*, p. 158.

[17]   Jeremy Bentham "Pannomial Fragments" in *The Works of Jeremy Bentham*, vol. III, p. 211.

[18]   Jeremy Bentham "General View of a Complete Code of Laws" in *Complete Works of Jeremy Bentham*, vol. III, p. 209. "I have endeavored to throw the burden upon the legislator, that the yoke might be lightened for the people. I have given the labour to the strong, that the repose of the weak may be better secured".

after the codification. The head of the hydra of unwritten law should be cut off, and the wound cauterized. In order to achieve this end one principal rule of interpretation and application of law should be applied which Bentham put into the following words: " . . . the text of the law should be the standard of the law."[19]

This sentence at first appears to be some kind of a definition *per idem*, but indeed it contains a very important indication and instructions. It means first of all that it is the text of the law and nothing else, which determines whether a given case falls within the law. A judge can, and should, devise a remedy where he finds a gap in the code but no decision of a judge, or of any other individual or expert "should be allowed to be cited as law,"[20] until the legislator himself has embodied the case fall within the law.

It may well be that a particular provision "appears at first sight to be repugnant to one more general"; "these two provisions should either be reconciled, or, if this be impossible, the particular provision should prevail over the general.[21]

Bentham understood that there may be contradictions even in the best of codes. In such a case the first reaction of a jurist should be that the contradiction is only apparent, an illusion, of "first sight," due rather to the weakness of our, and not of the legislator's, mind. The interpreters' presumption should be that the legislator had been reasonable, had been striving to achieve the greatest happiness for the greatest number, he did not want any contradictions. This presumption should be regarded as one of the principal maxims determining interpretation. One can ask another simple and logical question here: can the law be explained? Bentham was unable to give a consistent answer to this question.

In the same chapter (No. 34: "Of the interpretation, conservation and improvement of a code," in his essay, "General view of a complete Code of Laws,") he gave two dissimilar answers.

When Bentham stressed that the text of the law should be the chief object of attention, he added: "the examples which may be given being designed only to *explain*, not to *restrain*, the purport of law."[22]

In the next sentence he already withdrew partially from the concept of explanation: "one should not pay attention," he warned, "to any commentaries on the code, nothing should be allowed to be quoted in the court concerning the sense of the text."

As if this warning were insufficient, Bentham added the following phrase at the end of his pamphlet: "When, however, a passage appears to be obscure, let it be cleared up rather by alteration than by comment."[23]

---

[19] *Ibid.*, pp. 33–34; 40; 82–84.
[20] *Ibid.*, p. 210.
[21] *Ibid.*
[22] *Ibid.*
[23] *Ibid.*

Let us recapitulate Bentham's commentaries:
- when the text is clear, one may give examples in order to *explain* the text;
- explanations should be exemplifications only, but not explanations of the text, and all commentaries should be regarded mischievous or useless;
- what is truly obscure should not be explained, but referred to the legislator.

In reading this text, it seems that Bentham misunderstood one of the basic philosophical questions in the sphere of interpretation: nothing is clear *eo ipso* or *per se*, and every explanation or clarification is indeed an interpretation. It seems that Bentham was under the impression, partially caused by the Cartesian *Discourse on Method*, that one could see the essence clearly and distinctly even without a rhetorical discussion prior to the process of *understanding*.

On the other hand, when Bentham wrote about the problem of clarity not in direct connection with jurisprudence, but from the general philosophical viewpoint, he showed his non-Cartesian, rhetorical, understanding of the problem. In his *Essay on Logic* he concluded:

Clearness is, on every occasion, relative. . . . There exists not, nor ever will exist, any proposition that is perfectly clear to every hearer and reader. There exist but too many that neither will be, nor ever have been to any one. . . .[24]

How can we explain a relatively unclear text? Bentham gave one more answer in the rhetorical spirit: through discourse; and he noted that "*clearness* has for its *instrument, exposition.*"[25] (Italics – M.M.)

The immediate subject of every exposition is a word; but a "*word is only a sign of thought.*"[26]

Every exposition supposes thought[27] and it must be clarified in the process of discourse. The field of law, Bentham stressed in his *Essay on Logic*, is the field in which the exposition of thought is "most copious and most urgent, and the use of it most conspicuous and incontestable."[28]

What are the reasons for Bentham's inconsistencies, hesitations, and outright contradictions in his theory of interpretation of legal norms? Perhaps the explanation is: Bentham sensed that there was a need to introduce into jurisprudence the method which he called a Socratic mode, being different from

---

[24]   Jeremy Bentham: *Essay on Logic*, in *The Works*, vol. VIII, p. 242a.

[25]   *Ibid.*, p. 242b. Cf. also pp. 245, 251–252.

[26]   *Ibid.*

[27]   *Ibid.*, Cf. also 243–244 and *Essay on Language*, in *The Works*, vol. VIII, pp. 304–305.
"The greater the number is of the words that are employed in the expression of a given import, the *less clear* is the discourse which they compose" –*Ibid.*, p. 305a.
Clearness defines Bentham as an "exemption from ambiguity, and . . . obscurity" p. 304a. Obscurity he defines as "the superlative . . . ambiguity" or "ambiguity . . . to the widest extent" p. 305a.

[28]   *Ibid.*, vol. VIII, p. 243b.

Aristotle's logic but similar to rhetorical dialogue; but Bentham was unable (as were Holmes and Dewey a hundred years later) to make the decisive leap and consciously and consistently incorporate the rhetorical approach into his own way of thinking. Bentham's visions and inconsistencies prove how *desirable the rhetorical revival has become.*

Bentham also felt constrained by political motives. He was afraid that rhetoric could give more freedom than logic to the judges and administrators whom he did not trust. This is one of the illusions concerning the role of the logic which has been cultivated by logicians themselves. But toward the end of his life Bentham began to move quicker in the right direction, toward rhetorical thinking.

4. *Evidence and rhetoric*

In his monumental work *Rationale of Judicial Evidence, Specially Applied to English Practice,*[29] the rhetorical elements are already evident.

Logical or mathematical methods, wrote Bentham, are unfortunately inapplicable to the judicial purpose, because one cannot strictly define degrees of trustworthiness or untrustworthiness with a *fixed top* or *fixed bottom.*[30] There must be a subjective element in evaluating all evidence, because it is more or less determined by persuasion. The different votes of the members of the jury are frequently the result "of degrees of persuasion."[31]

Even when the judge is one person only, he can have a hard time making a decision because the contending forces are fighting in his mind. The Roman judge, argued Bentham, could have said: *Non liquet – just grounds of decision being wanting to me, I will not decide.* Unfortunately, Bentham regretted, the English judge does not have such freedom.[32]

The *probative force* of evidence, Bentham argued, depends on many objective and subjective elements which are taken into account "in human discourse"[33] and one should know them in order to understand what "influences the foundation of *affirmative* and *disaffirmative* persuasion."[34]

The mere concept of evidence is for Bentham "a word of relation"; this term means "any matter of fact, the effect, tendency, or design which, when presented to the mind, is to produce a *persuasion* (Italics – M.M.) – concerning the existence of some other matter of fact . . . "[35]

---

[29] *The Works of Jeremy Bentham*, ed., John Bowring, vols. VI and VII. Many of Bentham's basic ideas were presented in an abbreviated form in *"An Introductory View of the Rationale of Evidence: For the Use of Non-Lawyer as well as Lawyer.* Ibid., vol. VI.

[30] Jeremy Bentham, *An Introductory View of the Rationale of Evidence*, in *The Works*, vol. VI, p. 16. Cf. also: *Rationale of Judicial Evidence*, vol. VI, pp. 208, especially the problems of evidence in mathematics and experimental science.

[31] *Ibid.*

[32] *Ibid.*, vol. VI, p. 17.

[33] Vol. VI, p. 18.

[34] *Ibid.*, vol. VI, p. 18.

[35] *Rationale of Judicial Evidence* . . . vol. VI, p. 208.

As if he wrote under the direct influence of *Rhetoric*, Bentham added in the footnote that in "the word evidence (together with its conjugates, to *evidence, evidencing, evidenced*, and *evidentiary*) the English language possesses an instrument of discourse peculiar to itself: at least as compared with the Latin and French languages."[36]

Here once more we see how far Bentham was from the classical concept of truth as *adequatio rei et intellectus*. Truth and evidence do not speak for themselves and their probative force depends on the circumstances, among which, as was later observed by Perelman, the quality of the audience is decisive. Bentham called this factor "the public mind at its present state culture."[37] In this way Bentham once more cleared the scene for the *long awaited entrance of the art of argumentation*.

Bentham gave the following example: it could happen that a plaintiff's evidence, "forthcoming" and "standing alone," i.e., without a defendant's counter-evidence failed "to obtain the necessary *credence*," or the counter-evidence obtained the "stronger credence"; or it was found by the judge that in the evidence adduced by the defendant was "something of *incorrectness*, or partially operating incompleteness."[38]

In all these three examples the element of subjectivity, of persuasion and argumentation, is involved. Especially the notions of "correctness" or "completeness" are – Bentham understood it very well – rhetorical; their persuasive force depends on the arguments in which they are "wrapped" and presented; their validity depends on "power over language."[39]

Bentham reached the peak of his rhetorical considerations when he concluded: "*Veracity*, therefore, not less than *mendacity*, is the result of *interest*; and in so far as depends upon the *will*, it depends in each instance, upon the effect of the conflict between two opposite groups of contending interests, which of them shall be the result."[40]

Interest colors the qualities of the evidence and – as Bentham stressed – interest is reflected in the sphere of legislation and judge-made law.[41] The actual ends of the judicature in England, he stressed, representing improper or false ends,[42] are determined by the "private . . . personal . . . sinister interest of the monarch,"[43] such as money, power, reputation, vengeance.[44]

---

[36] *Ibid.*, vol. VI, p. 208.

[37] *Ibid.*, vol. VI, p. 17.

[38] *Ibid.*, vol. VI, p. 8.

[39] *The Works*, vol. VI, p. 22. Cf. also: ". . . experience is not sufficient always to open eyes that have been closed by prejudice . . ." in *"Rationale of Judicial Evidence"*, vol. VI, p. 206.

[40] *Ibid.*, vol. VI, p. 19.

[41] *Ibid.*, vol. VI, pp. 6, 8, 10.

[42] Bentham, *op. cit.*, vol. VI, p. 10.

[43] Bentham, *op. cit.*, vol. VI, p. 10.

[44] ". . . reputation, when operating upon an extensive scale, (is) called *fame* –" *Ibid.*, pp. 10–11.

The interest of the monarch was joined by the imbecility and mental vigor of the monarch's "instruments and substitutes, the judges."[45]

Their "sinister interests" also started to develop and "the seat of the sinister interest . . . (was) gradually shifting," but "the shapes in which it operated (are) still the same."[46] The judges' position and judge-made law are "fruits of scientifically and diligently cultivated delay, vexation, and expense."[47] There is not more justice in this law than piety in Trent's ecclesiastical law.

In this precarious situation, the evidence will be pondered, and especially the qualities of correctness and completeness, (being qualities "of the first order, qualities intrinsically desirable"[48] by the courts). But we cannot, wrote Bentham, form a *perfectly correct* conception of those qualities. Why?

"By *correctness*, therefore, must on this occasion, be understood – not *absolute*, but *relative* correctness; – by *correctness*, not *absolute*, but *relative* completeness: – in other words, by *correctness*, that and that alone, which is for its opposite, deceptions, incompleteness.[49]

Once correctness and completeness are only relative, what is the truth? It is "relative correctness and completeness."[50]

How can we achieve truth, even if relative? Bentham's answer is very clear: through *discourse*. Such a *discourse* can be, of course, let us add, only a *rhetorical* one. In such a discourse nothing has a constant value, as we know. Everything is always contestable; the evidentiary value of any fact depends on its relations with other facts, which are also contestable. What is regarded a "fact" can change its sense, because all facts are "feigned" and having this in mind we must answer the question whether "the supposed evidentiary facts afford a sufficient ground for being *persuaded* (Bentham's emphasis) of the corresponding existence of the principal facts,"[51] because the *same* matter of fact presented to the mind from one point of view, is not the *same* matter of fact when presented from another point of view; are these "two" matters of fact identical? asked Bentham. Can such a fact serve as a means to an end? After all, every evidence is merely "a means to an end," because it is "subservient" towards a course of action with some particular object in view.[52] How can we solve this problem?

Once more we are given the same recommendation: the method of solution is discourse, this is the way to achieve the most "truthful," "relative," truth.

The attempt to analyze the activity of the government on judicial evidence remains to this hour "a perfect blank," because: "Power has hitherto kept it in a state of wilderness: reason has never visited it."[53]

45   Bentham, *Ibid.*, p. 11.
46   Bentham, *Ibid.*, p. 11.
47   Bentham, *op. cit.*, VI, 9.
48   *Ibid.*, vol. VI, p. 21.
49   *Ibid.*, vol. VI. p. 21 (all emphasis by Bentham).
50   *Ibid.*, vol. VI. p. 22.
51   *Ibid.*, vol. VI. p. 203.
52   *Ibid.*, vol. VI. p. 209a.

In this gloomy situation prevailing in the fields of politics and justice, rhetorical discourse seems to be our last hope and escape.

This analysis of Bentham's philosophy of law, including his theory of evidence, was an attempt to explain that the founder of juridical positivism was aware that one had to return to "Socratic Modes" in order to move forward. He, himself, started to leave the narrow premises of formal logic and began to move towards rhetoric.

The rediscovery and development of the rhetorical theory of argumentation by Chaim Perelman gives a new incentive to the further development of jurisprudence. Today western jurisprudence needs more than ever the help of the new "critical rationalism" that transcends exaggerated duality: "judgments of reality, value judgments."[54]

In the copious field of law and jurisprudence – if I may use the style of Bentham – the need for the new rhetorical theory of argumentation is today incontestable. The new symbiosis of philosophy and positivist jurisprudence on the rhetorical basis "that is neither compelling nor arbitrary" can "give meaning to human freedom,"[55] to human rights, to certainty, order, and to a reasonable exercise of choices.

The American founders of the legal philosophy were familiar with the writings of Bentham. Therefore, they were able to go faster than their European counterparts toward rhetorical approach and to go beyond formal logic.

B. THE NEW RHETORIC AND AMERICAN JURISPRUDENCE

The purpose of this chapter is to compare American legal philosophy with the new theory of argumentation developed by Chaim Perelman. Our analysis can be summarized in the following way: Oliver Wendell Holmes, Benjamin Cardozo, John Dewey and many other eminent representatives of American philosophy and jurisprudence found that in order to develop their ideals and theories, they had to go beyond the formal logic of syllogisms. They began to search for new methods but they never did solve the problem. The answer that they sought, however, was provided by Professor Chaim Perelman and his theory of argumentation.

Here we will concentrate chiefly on the problems of jurisprudence and morality in connection with rhetorical argumentation. We will first analyze the respective ideas of the American authors, then we will show how the New Rhetoric is an organic and logical continuation of certain trends in jurisprudence.

---

[53] *Rationale of Judicial Evidence*, vol. VI, p. 209b.
[54] Ch. Perelman & L. Abrechts-Tyteca. *The New Rhetoric* (University of Notre Dame Press, Notre Dame-London, 1971), p. 514.
[55] *Ibid.*

1. *Oliver Wendell Holmes: logic and good sense*

It is a fact that in the twentieth century most eminent representatives of American jurisprudence have found that formal logic alone is inadequate for the explanation, interpretation, and application of legal norms, either statutes or the common law. For many social, economic, and political reasons, Americans realized long before their European counterparts that the life of the law cannot rest on the logic of syllogisms alone. Why the Americans have the priority in this field is a topic for a special study, not pertinent to our theme.

From the very beginning of his practical and theoretical activity, Justice Oliver Wendell Holmes helped to lay down the premises for the new juridical methodology.

In the lectures on "Agency" which were delivered in 1891, Holmes asserted "that the whole outline of law is the resultant of a conflict at every point between logic and good sense – the one striving to work fiction out to consistent results, the other restraining and at last overcoming that effort when the results become too manifestly unjust."[56]

Could this sentence be interpreted as a condemnation of the use of logic, or of common sense? Is there really an unbridgeable chasm between the two? It would appear that Holmes wanted merely to state that an indiscriminate use of formal logic (the logic of syllogisms) could lead to "manifestly unjust" consequences and that therefore in the process of interpreting and applying the law we should use tools other than formal logic. We should not abandon logic, but we should not expect or demand too much from the rigorous use of syllogisms.

Should we, on the other hand, decisively turn to "good sense" and rely mainly on it to solve legal problems? This policy would not be advisable either. "Good" or "common" sense is often identified with "natural justice" or "natural law" and vice versa. Holmes' critical remarks about "natural law" should be applied to "good sense" as well: "The jurists who believe in natural law seem to me to be in that naive state of mind that accepts what has been familiar and accepted by them and their neighbors as something that must be accepted by all men everywhere."[57]

The conflict between formal "logic" and "good sense" (which usually presents itself under natural reason or law), according to Holmes, sometimes becomes a conflict between an alleged consistency of logic (indeed, leading to injustice) and the naiveté of familiar convictions.

Legal norms should not be treated like abstract mathematical axioms because law is directly connected with the real conflicts of life.

But the provisions of the constitution are not mathematical formulae having

---

[56]   Oliver Wendell Holmes, *Collected Legal Papers* (New York: Peter Smith, 1952), p. 50.
[57]   *Ibid.*, p. 312.

their essence in their form; they are organic living institutions . . . Their significance is vital not formal; it is to be gathered not simply by taking the words and a dictionary, but by considering their origin and the line of their growth.[58]

What is "vital" should not be treated like a "dead letter," or like a formula for life which is reduced to its "form." Law is a response to our aspirations, to the experience of mankind, is not reducible to a formula whose meaning has been pre-determined. Mere reading of the legal norms is not sufficient; it is equally necessary to consider their whole line of growth as well. One should start at the beginning, but only in order to realize fully that law, as the "witness and external deposit" of our lives, registers the moral development of society.[59] For this reason, an uncritical or dogmatic application of formal logic to the living organism of the law brings about results which are repellent from the human viewpoint.

And yet, after numerous criticisms of the insufficiency of logic, we find Holmes making the following statement: "The training of lawyers is a training in logic. The process of analogy, discrimination, and deduction is mainly the language of logic."[60]

These words were to become famous in juridical literature to indicate how important logic is in legal training.[61]

Strictly speaking, Holmes' notion of formal logic differs from that usually accepted in our time. Discrimination and analogy are foreign to formal logic. Nevertheless, the fact that Holmes treated formal logic more broadly does not alter the tenor of our remarks.

In an address delivered to the Supreme Court of Massachusetts in 1897, Holmes stressed how vain was the conviction of those who looked for certainty in the application of logic to law:

And the logical method and form flatter that longing for certainty and for repose which is in every human mind. But certainty generally is illusion, and repose is not the destiny of man.[62]

The above is one of his most important observations concerning the importance of logic in legal practice: logic creates the illusion of certainty; actually such certainty does not exist and cannot be attained. Even should it exist to a certain degree, it would not owe its existence to the logic of syllogisms.

The most damaging illusion, however, is the illusion that legal conclusions based on logic are free from subjectivity, that they are completely

---

[58] Gompers v. U.S., 233 U.S. 604, (1913). In *The Holmes Reader*, p. 205.
[59] Holmes "The Path of the Law," *Collected Legal Papers, ibid.*, p. 170.
[60] *Ibid.*, p. 181.
[61] *The Holmes Reader*, p. 209.
[62] Holmes, *Collected Legal Papers*, p. 181.

detached from the individual who harbors them; that they have a life of their own. The contrary is true. As Holmes writes:

> Behind the logical form lies a judgment as to the relative worth and importance of competing legislative grounds, often an inarticulate and unconscious judgment, it is true, and yet the very root and nerve of the whole proceeding. You can give any conclusion a logical form.[63]

Legal conclusions can always be given in a logical form. It is for this reason that lawyers are trained in logic. This is not to say that they are not to be trained to apply logic to the interpretation of legal norms (such application very often becomes impossible when the quantitative measurements are not known), instead they learn how to present their own subjective conclusions in an objective, impersonal, logical form. Training in logic does not pertain to the essence of professional activity in the field of law, but to the manner and form of legal presentation: subjectivity must be presented as objectivity.

These considerations do not make a good case for formal logical thought in the sphere of law. And because one is not able to reach an exact logical conclusion in a given case, one's conclusions

> . . . can do no more than embody the preference of a given body in a given time and place. We do not realize how large a part of our law is open to reconsideration upon a slight change in the habit of the public mind. No concrete proposition is self-evident; no matter how ready we may be to accept it.[64]

Such is the essence of Holmes' view of the role of logic in jurisprudence. Every judicial decision (not concerned with technical problems such as data), apart from its logical form, embodies the philosophical or political preference of a given body rather than a determination drawn from the "iron logic," which supposedly is the only one correct, certain, and absolute expression of absolute justice. On the contrary: juridical decisions are subjective because they reflect the personal preference of the author who has his own ideas and is also subject to the influence of the changing moods and opinions of the public.

"No concrete proposition is self-evident . . . " this means that a proposition must seek the adherence of the minds of one's hearers. The so-called compelling force of self-evidence, obviousness, rationality, and logical consistency, are not sufficient in themselves. One must use the force of argument to persuade those at whom the arguments are directed. This last conclusion was never expressed by Holmes in such a clear way, but it is inherent in his method of thinking. It portends the great leap from the realm of formal logic to the realm of argumentation.

Holmes did not leave one stone on another in destroying illusions about

---

[63] *Ibid.*
[64] *Ibid.*, p. 181.

the role of syllogisms in law. But he did not have anything to replace formal logic so that reasonableness in juridical practice would be assured.

The ground for the New Theory of Argumentation was cleared by Holmes. But it was John Dewey who added new dimensions to this analysis.

2. *John Dewey on "Other", "Experimental" and "Flexible" logic*

In his essay, "Logical Method and Law," John Dewey analyzes Holmes' ideas about the place of logic in the interpretation of law. Dewey concludes that whenever Holmes uses the words, in his legal writings, "logic" and "logical," he means "formal logic," logic as "formal consistency," the consistency of "concepts . . . irrespective of the consequences of their application to concrete matters-of-fact."[65]

Jurists are inclined to use the ready-made, familiar, concepts of logic, because it is convenient and economical for them to do so. No further effort is required to devise a new pattern; furthermore, recourse to logic gives rise "to a sense of stability, of a guarantee against sudden and arbitrary changes of the rules."[66] One should be wary of this use of logic, and "a sound logic" will guard against it.

Dewey views formal logic, or the logic of syllogisms, as a logic which is not "sound" (concerning application to law, morality, and politics). But what is a "sound" logic? Here Dewey's explanations are meager. He does, however, make an important comment regarding Holmes' famous expression: "The actual life of law has not been logic: it has been experience."[67]

Dewey understands that here Holmes uses the word logic in the traditional orthodox way, meaning the logic of syllogisms and Dewey stresses that there exists an antithesis between such logic and experience, between this logical and good sense. Consequently, there is a need for "another kind of logic."[68]

This "other" logic would not assert that reason has "fixed forms of its own" anterior to the subject matter, to which "the latter have to be adapted."[69] Orthodox logic is a logic of "rigid demonstration," but not of "search and discovery," Dewey states. The logic of syllogisms pays no attention to the social consequences of decisions made with its help.

---

[65]   John Dewey, *Philosophy and Civilization* (New York: Minton, Batchand Co., 1931), p. 130.

[66]   *Ibid.*, p. 131.

[67]   This sentence is one of the first to appear in the book by Holmes, *The Common Law*. Later one reads: "The felt necessities of the time, the prevalent moral and political theories, intuitions of public policy, avowed or unconscious, even the prejudices which the judges share with their fellow-men, have a good deal more to do than the syllogism in determining the rules by which men should be governed. This embodies the story of a nation's development through many centuries, and it cannot be dealt with as if it contained only the axioms and corollaries of a book of mathematics." (Cambridge: The Belknap Press of Harvard University Press, Mass., 1963), p. 5.

[68]   John Dewey, *op. cit.*, p. 132.

[69]   *Ibid.*

What can be said of the "other" kind of logic which Dewey recommends? It will be a logic which will reduce the influence of habit; it will facilitate the use of good sense; it will take into account the social consequences of legal decisions; it will deal with the *operations* of thought and not only with its *results*; it will not arrogate to itself the presumption that every possible case which may arise can be resolved simply on the basis of a fixed antecedent rule.

According to formal logic, a logical conclusion "subsumes" a particular under an appropriate general principle; nothing more need be said.

According to the "other kind of logic," general rules do not mechanically decide concrete cases; nothing necessarily follows automatically from general statements or general legal rules. General rules can only act as "generic ways" which may aid in solving any given question.

Dewey calls this "other logic" an "experimental logic,"[70] a "sound" logic, a "vital" logic,[71] and finally the "logic of inquiry,"[72] because it is "flexible."[73]

The use of the "logic of inquiry" does not reduce "predictability" in the sphere of law. Quite the contrary: theoretical certainty will be replaced by practical certainty.[74] Social needs will be met because the logic of inquiry relates to consequences and not to antecedents.[75]

There is a gap, Dewey writes, between antecedents and the new requirements of life. Whoever uses antecedents alone must do so in an arbitrary manner covered with syllogisms.

Those who use "experimental logic," however, are more *creative*, more oriented toward reality and give more assurance that the law will be applied as regularly as possible. "Gambling" with old rules does not increase "practical certainty," but instead serves the "virtual alliance between the judiciary and entrenched interests."[76] Such are the social characteristics of the "logic of inquiry," as understood by Dewey. This logic serves to promote progress, it is basically creative and liberal; it is oriented toward social justice.

Moreover, this "vital logic" takes into account the fact that "the personal element cannot wholly be excluded"[77] from judicial decisions. But how can such a "subjective" decision preserve its authority, its aura of objectivity? The answer can only be through introduction of the element of the public and its enlightened opinion. The absence of the latter element is what separates Dewey's "logic of inquiry" from the new theory of argumentation as applied to jurisprudence, propounded by Perelman.

Holmes proved that logic of syllogisms can lead to unreasonable inhumane results. Dewey proved that formal logic can support "the bulwarks of

---

[70]   *Ibid.*, p. 133.
[71]   *Ibid.*, p. 136.
[72]   *Ibid.*, p. 139.
[73]   *Ibid.*, p. 140.
[74]   *Ibid.*, p. 136.
[75]   *Ibid.*, p. 138.
[76]   *Ibid.*, p. 139.
[77]   *Ibid.*, p. 136.

reaction."[78] He subsequently elaborated his logic of experience and – against the prevailing philosophical mood – he started to consider the reasonable of moral norms. In this way, Dewey advanced half a step further toward rhetorical logic and argumentation.

In the "Afterword" (1946) to his book, *The Public and Its Problems* (first published in 1927), Dewey makes the following remarks concerning moral norms and their social value:

> . . . in order to interest the citizens . . . in an actual war, it has been necessary to carry on a campaign to show that superior moral claims were on the side of a war policy. The change of attitude is not fundamentally an affair of moral conversion, a change from obdurate immorality to a perception of the claims of righteousness. It results from greatly intensified recognition of the factual consequences of war.[79]

From Dewey's point of view, as expressed in one of his last writings, what is moral or immoral does not depend on any unchangeable, absolute moral category; it depends on public understanding and the perception of what should be regarded as proper (moral, just) way of acting. According to the absolutistic philosophies of morality and truth, when one party supports a war and a second opposes it, only one can represent the requirements of morality and justice; the other must be sunk in "obdurate immorality." Once we admit the public's opinion into the spectrum of our evaluation, the results of our analysis will be broader, deeper, more flexible (by this we do not mean more eclectic), more humane. Both factions, pro- and anti-war, may represent moral and social values at least for a time. When the dialogue goes on, when new facts about the conduct of the war and behaviour of the aggressors become known, when the public becomes more and more persuaded by the old and the new arguments of the pro-war faction – then, more and more people will perceive who represents "*superior* moral claims." (italics – M.M.) From the absolutistic, dogmatic viewpoint, a change of moral attitude implies a "moral conversion." Not so, says Dewey. In this respect, his theory coincides with the New Rhetoric. New moral awareness and a change of mind are a normal, non-revolutionary, development resulting from the public dialogue. It also means that opposition to war may become morally untenable at a certain point, although for a while it may have been regarded morally justifiable. The majority will view their political adversaries as representatives of "obdurate immorality." At any rate, the moral, or immoral, has no absolute content.

In this manner, Dewey made one more turn toward the revival of the rhetorical tradition.

---

[78]   *Ibid.*, p. 139.
[79]   John Dewey, "Afterword" in *The Public and its Problems* (Chicago: The Swallow Press, 1954), p. 224.

C. RHETORICAL THEORY OF THE INTERPRETATION OF LAW

1. *Juridical craft or legal philosophy?*

The results of the 1987 Senate hearings on the nomination of Judge Robert Bork to the U.S. Supreme Court pose a very basic question: is it possible to master the juridical craft without any philosophy, ethics, or even elementary human feelings? Is it possible for a juridical "craftsman" or "technician," to discharge his legal duties properly? Can there be any such thing as a good judge who has no philosophical horizons, moral convictions, or compassion?

The criticism of Judge Robert Bork in well-publicized opinions pertains not only to his philosophy but also to his approach to interpretation and application of the law. The art of juridical interpretation is not a mechanical skill. To interpret the law properly and then to apply the general norm to a concrete individual situation, is a creative process which engages all the intellectual powers of a jurist. The conclusions of a judge's reasoning are not arrived at by deduction, by "axiomatic reasoning" aided by "pure reason" and formal logic. On the contrary, so many elements enter into a judge's reasoning combined with social and moral percepts that any pretensions to infallibility must be excluded.

Western jurisprudence long ago discarded Montesquieu's simplistic recommendation that a judge should not interpret, but only act as "the mouthpiece of the law." Western jurisprudence consequently has elaborated many sophisticated methods and norms of interpretation and application of law.

Unfortunately, familiarity with the art of legal interpretation is not reflected in Judge Bork's writings, opinions, or responses to the Senate Committee. For instance, he uncritically adopts the idea of "original intent," although he should know that he is merely oversimplifying the European theory of the "subjective will" of the legislator. The European "subjectivists" at one time were criticized by "objectivists" who argued that a judge must be guided not by the unclear, uncertain, and ultimately unknowable "will" of the legislator, but by the objective meaning of the legal norms as expressed in the legal text. During the long battles between the two camps the positions shifted and ultimately both parties borrowed arguments and constructions from one another. Lastly, some of the "subjectivists" became more "objectivistic" than their opponents, and vice versa.

Politicians who talk about the "original will" are not required to know the history of this theory. Judge Bork, and his powerful conservative adherents however, should have been more discriminating about this old idea in new accouterments. Had they even once referred to the voluminous literature about this subject, they would have found that the entire concept of "original intent" falls apart. They would then not have expressed the totally unfounded opinion that lacking this theory a judge would find himself like a boat without a rudder, the prey of arbitrary impulses.

Indeed, during the Senate hearings, Bork contradicted himself in the historically meaningful discussion with Senator Arlin Spencer.

When Judge Bork interpreted presidential powers in an expansive way and argued that the Constitution left room for its "organic development" Senator Spencer retorted: "Why only organic development for executive power and not for the Bill of Rights?"

The essence of the contradictions between the line of reasoning represented by Bork and his supporters, and those who disagree with them can be narrowed down to the following. Nowadays, the New American Right interprets functions and privileges of executive power expansively but narrowly interprets the Bill of Rights and other Amendments to the Constitution. Their adversaries, however, regard rights and freedoms a point of departure of the Constitution and the goal of its interpretation and realization.

These faults in the New Rights' reasoning are a key to the denial of the right to privacy. Although this expression is not explicitly used in the Constitution, its correct interpretation nevertheless indicated that an individual is given a whole congeries of rights, which like a garment surround and protect him. These rights constitute a "zone of rights" (Justice Douglas). Without these rights the very concept of freedom would become meaningless. The philosophical concept of privacy accords with the spirit and letter of the Constitution and whoever denies this is neither a "strict constructionist" nor a supporter of "judicial restraint." He does opt, however, for the eradication of the soul of the Constitution, which is freedom. When, in connection with *Griswold* and *Roe* Judge Bork and other ideologues of the New Right write that the Court had unjustifiably usurped the states' authority, one can answer that the contrary has occurred: certain branches of the government unconstitutionally usurped authority in the domain of individual choice.

Today, in addition to the Constitution, we live in an era of the Universal Declaration of Human Rights. The following philosophical directive consequently seems appropriate in the interpretation of the Constitution: in the event of doubt, one should opt for American liberties and individual rights. This is also the point of departure of the rhetorical theory of legal interpretation.

It is difficult to be a good jurist and correctly exercise one's juridical craft without adhering to that basic philosophy of a democratic society.

2. Basic rhetorical principles of legal interpretation

The use of formal logic to interpret the law cannot by itself assure stability or certainty. If, however, a law is the result of legislative doubletalk, then nothing logicians can do will clarify where clarity was never intended. In such a situation logic can be used, or rather abused, to produce more uncertainty.

Sometimes laws are obsolete and are regarded as antisocial by much of society. When that is true, a strictly logical interpretation and application can be disruptive and cause disorder and uncertainty rather than stability.

The institution of *lettres de cachet* in prerevolutionary France, "strictly" and "logically" applied could have had but one effect: indignation, fear, and revolution – indeed it is absurd to apply "logic" and rules of juridical interpretation to "laws" concerning *lettres de cachet*. According to Stalinist law the verdict of a secret tribunal consisting of three officers of the security police was final; the tribunals acted on the basis of a record produced by lower security officers.

Neither the defendant nor his lawyer (defense counsel was almost unheard of) had any right to appear before this tribunal; defendants could not offer evidence or explanations of any kind. Death sentences under that law were almost immediately executed.

In such a juridical situation, what good is it to emphasize "logic and obedience to written law?" In inhuman circumstances formal logic and "obedience to written law" aggravate the cruelty and add insult to injury.

There are many good reasons to argue that the decision in the case of Dred Scott was logically faultless. But it was inhumane. One could argue that the decision of the court was discordant with the Constitution of the United States. In hindsight, that is true. But for three quarters of a century slavery and the Constitution were regarded compatible.

It was not formal logic applied to the interpretation of the Constitution which changed that abominable situation. One must use more "subtle" instruments to interpret the law in order to prove the incompatibility of slavery, and of other institutions that today are considered unjust, with the Constitution. It is rhetorical thinking that must be applied; it presupposes another type of philosophy and *Weltanschauung*.

A general philosophy which one accepts more or less consciously, can determine the attitudes of the people, their behavior, choices, decisions, biases, prejudices, and inclinations to a certain degree only. A philosophy of law is more down to earth than a general philosophy, at the same time being an integral part of a general philosophy; it is a part of the general *Weltanschauung*. As such it also flies high and is one of the sources of general moral and social precepts. On the other hand, being general and particular at the same time, a philosophy of law can influence the general attitudes and ways of thinking of jurists and politicians and can influence the interpretation and application of law. As a matter of fact, in every important, rather than technical, decision made by jurists the philosophical, ideological, *Weltanschalich* attitude is influential.

One of the tasks of a rhetorical philosophy of law is to convert an unconscious dependence on philosophy and morality into a conscious one in the process of selecting values while interpreting and applying the law.

A narrow view of juridical interpretation is one of the products of the narrow understanding of legal positivism, but it is not legal positivism itself that should be held responsible for that.

According to the New Rhetoric, one should combine the general principles of law with justice, equity, and common sense to achieve reasonable and justifiable determinations without violating the provisions of the law in force and at the same time fill the gaps.

In order to achieve such a result, we must consider the legal provisions *in toto*, all parts of the law, not only selected portions. Lord Coke, therefore, "considers the preamble as a key to open the understanding of the Statute."[80]

A preamble can be helpful in ascertaining the true meaning of a juridical act. To be specific, the preamble can be resorted to "in restraint of the generality of the enacting clause, when it would be inconvenient if not restrained."[81] (Kent, *Commentaries*, I).

The second reason why a preamble may be useful is to explain "the enacting clause, if it be doubtful."[82]

Let us briefly remark that it is possible to be a juridical positivist and consider that the sources of law are not only normative, but also normal "prose," the prose of Mr. Jourdain, when used in preambles or in introductions explaining the intentions of the legislator.

Kent distinguishes between the real and the literal sense of a statute. He writes:

> The true meaning of the statute is generally and properly to be sought from the body of the act itself . . . It is an established rule in the exposition of statutes, that the intention of the law giver is to be deduced from a view of the whole and of every part of a statute, taken and compared together. The real intention, when accurately ascertained, will always prevail over the literal sense of the terms.

Is incompatibility between the "real" or "true" meaning of a statute and the "literal sense" unavoidable? Must such a problem emerge?

The rhetorical approach to the interpretation of law throws a special light on the problem of the "authentic" interpretation of law, that is, the interpretation made by the legislator himself. According to the old maxim: *eius est interpretari legem, cuius est condere*. If an authentic interpretation has power as binding as law itself, then the term "interpretation" is misleading, for indeed the legislator has issued a new law calling it an interpretation.

Considering the contents of the interpreted norms, there are three possibilities, according to Perelman's published and unpublished lectures:
1. The behavior prescribed by the "authentic interpretation" is exactly the same as that prescribed by the norm; or
2. The interpretation changes the behavior prescribed by the norm; or
3. The norm is so unclear that one cannot determine its meaning, and consequently a practical application of it is impossible without the interpretation.

---

[80] Roscoe Pound and Theodore F. T. Plucknett, *Readings on the History and System of the Common Law* (Rochester: The Lawyers Cooperative Publishing Company, 1927), p. 263.
[81] *Ibid.*
[82] *Ibid.*

If the "authentic" interpretation completely coincides with the norm, there is no need for it. But as far as practical jurists are concerned, any "official" interpretation is the source of additional trouble. If they believe in a dynamic theory of interpretation and feel that the legal provisions have objectively started to exist independently of their creator, should they then dig into the text of the law only, or should they also search for the "deeper" meaning of the norms in official interpretations?

If the interpretation changes the ascertained meaning of the norm in an obvious way, then the legislator has changed the law, but not in the usual way, not in good faith, and perhaps in a manner contrary to the constitution.

If the change in a law is not apparent, so that specialists are needed to detect the change, then one must conclude that the legislator was afraid to disclose his real intentions, that he was attempting to deceive his constituents. Laws in books usually survive their creators. Should successors be obliged to follow a false interpretation which was rendered *in male fide*? Should they not return to the original text of the law and put the interpretation aside?

The legislator's decision to issue his own "authentic" interpretation which is contrary to the law is always a political decision, inviting a political reaction against an allegedly juridical pronouncement. The result must be a debasement of law.

In such a case an additional interpretation is advisable, not to say necessary. Without this interpretation jurists would have to interpret norms through the use of the rules of interpretation. If in the process of interpreting an unclear norm the intention of the legislator is distorted, then only the legislator himself is to blame, but what about applying the maxim: *nullum crimen sine lege*?

Rhetorical conclusions concerning authentic interpretations do not in any way contradict one of our fundamental theses, that the meaning of legal norms by their nature is at the same time both determined and limitless, because every new set of circumstances gives us a new opportunity to refine and ascertain the meaning of a norm.

The legislator usually knows what he wants to express and he also knows what he does not want to say. But his influence on the objective meaning of the norm is limited because once he promulgates the norm it takes on an independent life. The legislator is bound by the meaning of the words he used to the same degree as any other citizen in the country.

When the norm becomes "independent," then the legislator himself, when he invokes it, must interpret it. He also faces the problem of what is clear and what is obscure in the process of applying this norm to the given case.

Is it necessary to interpret every juridical text on every occasion in order to apply it?

According to the Cartesian way of thinking the answer should be: I must interpret every text as long as it is necessary in order to understand it clearly and distinctly. When I reach this level of understanding, I can stop interpreting and start applying the clearly and distinctly understood provisions of law to the various situations to the facts.

The Cartesian approach gives rise to a perennial problem: is it possible to reach such a stage of clarity? Is clarity an objective state, or a subjective conviction? If it is subjective, then I am the person who decides when to stop interpreting and start applying a text. If it is an objective state, then, once again, a new question arises: how do we know when we have reached it? Such criteria, as we know, have not been found and unanimously accepted by all. In fact, they can never be found, but according to the principles of the New Rhetoric, one can argue *for* or *against* the criteria used in any given case. Whenever we face a new set of facts which need to be legally evaluated, we start by interpreting the relevant legal norms because in new circumstances no norms are clear or obvious from the rhetorical viewpoint.

One can generally argue that every juridical norm must be interpreted before it can be applied. Every legal norm is an abstraction and needs to be "brought down" to earth; it must be reduced to more simple elements in order to be able to come to grips with the facts of a particular case. Every application of law is connected with some kind of interpretation, although not every interpretation must be applied in practice. As Ch. B Nutting observes: "While students of semantics may explore the problem of 'meaning' at their leisure, courts must decide cases."[83]

Students of law, especially philosophers of law, can engage in endless disputes concerning the real meaning of a norm, but jurists – attorneys and judges – must decide the case before them, even in the midst of the most heated public controversy.

Philosophers and theologians, for instance, can engage in endless discussion about the origin of life, whether a fetus is a person, or whether life stops with the death of the brain or the beat of the heart, but the courts must decide such questions quickly, from a practical point of view, because it is their duty to do so and their failure to do so promptly affects the legitimate rights, liberties, and duties of others.

The courts cannot wait for the end of a discussion among scientists, moralists, and politicians; they must make their decisions according to their best knowledge and understanding at a given time, and in this way they contribute to the process of making the law objective.

The meaning they achieve is never absolute but only rhetorical; it is not static, but dynamic; it is not metaphysical, but dialectical; it is not established once and for all time, but is always a stage, a phase in an endless quest for clarity.

Therefore the maxim: *"interpretatio cessat in claris"* (interpretation stops when norms are clear) is itself unclear. But when can one say – argues Perelman – that a text is clear? When the sense which was given to the text by the legislator is clear? Who created the norms? When is the sense, actually given in the text, found clear by a judge? When do these two senses coincide? Indeed, such a coincidence is insufficient because the legal norm necessarily must

---

[83]   *Ibid.*

be interpreted within the context of the juridical system, and it can oblige one to resort to the reading of the text whose general clauses, while supporting the structure as a whole, are not quite clear.

Perelman's reasoning represents a crucial argument against the simplistic application of the maxim on "*interpretatio cessat in claris.*" If every legal rule must be interpreted in connection with the "spirit of the laws," the emergence of new doubts is unavoidable. After we start to reinterpret "clear" norms, those which are understood "clearly and distinctly," it will inevitably occur that the norm deemed clear is indeed more abstruse, has more than one meaning, and indicates more than one possible pattern of behavior. The mere act of subsuming facts to norms and vice versa, is conditioned by a set of juridical and social factors, including the general principles of law, the juridical culture of the society, the skill and traditions of the given legal community and the legal profession in general and the "sociological imagination" so highly appreciated by C. Wright Mills.

3. *Rhetorical maxim: in dubio pro iuribus hominis (when in doubt, decide in favor of human rights)*

Whoever feels that there can be only one rational interpretation and application of any given norm falls into the dogmatist's trap. The dogmatists and absolutists may be consistent and logical, but they are neither humane nor reasonable. *Errare humanum est!* The errors which result from discussion and arguments are not entirely unreasonable. But the errors which result from dogmatism, from "absolute" consistency and allegedly logical, rationalistic deductions may be entirely unreasonable, and even more: they can be devastatingly antihuman. What is reasonable can be false, but will always be more or less humane. What is absolutely logical can be a "crackpot" realism, can be inhuman and lead to deeds morally outrageous, if not outright criminal.

The basic philosophical directive in the contemporary interpretation and application of law can be expressed in the following way: all legal norms should be interpreted in such a way that human, democratic rights are not violated, but on the contrary, preserved and expanded.

The old Roman maxim: *in dubio pro reo*, should be changed: *in dubio pro iuribus hominis* (in case of doubt – decide in favor of human rights).

This concept is philosophical, juridical, moral, and political at the same time. It should be the humanists' credo!

And this is the basic rhetorical rule of the interpretation of law.

D. POSITIVIST REALISM AS A RHETORICAL PHILOSOPHY OF LAW

We live at a time when a new concept of law is evolving although it has not been theoretically assessed. One may call it positivist realism or rhetorical positivism.

Rhetorical positivism can be described as a philosophical amalgam of juridical positivism and American jurisprudence, international and municipal norms on human rights, and the philosophy and methodology of the New Rhetoric.

This realism emerges as a theory of law adjusted to the new social conditions and political realities of the end of the 20th century. It encompasses the traditions of the western philosophy of law and the experience of all modern societies. It is a theory of law that explains the nature of law and can aid the perennial struggle for democracy and peace, social order and human rights, international cooperation and sovereignty. This notion, like the Hegelian essence, tries to penetrate into the depth of important relationships hidden under the surface; positivist realism is not just a study of phenomena, whether they take the form of juridical norms or the behavior of lawyers. It studies phenomena as a first step toward understanding the substantial relationship between norms, morality, and behavior on the one hand, and social, economic, and political relationships on the other.

Virtually all states today (there are a few temporary exceptions) are members of the international community symbolized by the United Nations. They have all accepted the Charter of the United Nations as a valid legal document. Most of them also signed the Universal Declaration of Human Rights. All of them voted for the Declaration on Principles of International Law (1970). Almost half of the world's nations joined the International Covenants on Human Rights (1966). The provisions concerning human rights, as expressed in the Charter of the United Nations and in other documents are binding in various ways on the governments of all countries. It does not matter what a given government thinks about the relationship between international law and internal law; whether it considers that international law becomes part of internal law by its own authority or through some domestic legislative enactment, is irrelevant to our conclusions. The norms of international law as well as the general and specific provisions of the constitutions and other general legal acts, even of dictatorships, are a source of immunities, liberties, and subjective rights which cannot morally, or even legally, be denied or ignored.

Nobody today may claim that he adheres to the principles of due process of law while regarding democratic freedoms and subjective rights as empty and void. Rights and duties can, of course, be more or less general or specific. General legal provisions which are embodied in constitutions create very broad notions of rights which can be specified in legal acts of lower rank. They can be made more or less real; they can be expanded or abridged, but they cannot be – neither from the moral nor the juridical viewpoint – cancelled, liquidated, interpreted as being empty, or rendered null and void. Whenever the authorities try to curtail or nullify democratic liberties and rights, their attempts or acts are illegal because they violate the provisions of higher, basic, fundamental, legal acts and guarantees to which they themselves have adhered or at least promised to adhere.

In non-democratic states, particularly in the totalitarian ones, the facade of relatively democratic and progressive legal norms are all that exist as the last hope, the last life preserver that the oppressed citizens may look to. In totalitarian countries, constitutional and juridical pronouncements are almost like propaganda. The security police can violate these safeguards, liberties, and rights with impunity. But the virtue of a *legal positivist* attitude is evident here: the victim knows his rights and can claim them; the oppressor knows that he has violated the law; he must hide his violations, must consider public opinion, the weakness of his political regime, and the possibility of future punishment for himself, punishment which much more powerful violators than he have been unable to evade.

It is a modern paradox that the citizens of non-democratic countries can afford to ignore the law on the books even less than the citizens of traditional democracies can. They must abide by the traditional, and at the same time rhetorical, interpretation and application of positive law (including constitutional law), because any deviation from the letter of the law will be held against them and not against the powerful authorities.

Finally, it is the New Rhetoric which enables us to connect the two juridical doctrines: realism and positivism, until now regarded as intellectually divided.

A study of the writings of American legal realists as a whole leads to the conclusion that these American thinkers devised no new anti-positivistic philosophy of law, but rather promoted a development within positivistic philosophy, a tendency to assure maximum justice within a legal system which, according to Llewelyn, is in constant flux within the society, while the society itself is always changing too.

Even if, in their rebellion against traditional conceptualism, some "legal realists" rejected the traditional philosophy of law," that does not mean very much; a person's description of himself is not necessarily accurate.

The further the legal realists go from allegedly dogmatic, schematic, juridical positivism, the nearer they are to a non-dogmatic positivism, one which is more modern, more rhetorical, more grounded on experience, and less on syllogistic logic.

Let us reconsider at least one example and compare the social and political conditions in the U.S. at the end of the last century when the Supreme Court legalized the concept of "separate but equal" with the political climate in the 1950's when, in *Brown v. Board of Education*, the Supreme Court finally reversed itself, turning toward integration.

The weakness of a narrowly interpreted juridical positivism has been overcome only recently by combining juridical positivism with the positive expression of human rights and broadened by the new theory of argumentation.

Rhetorical positivism or positivist realism which is expounded in this volume is not a timeless theory of law. It presents the latest legal developments in their most general form and it provides a fruitful promise for the future.

It is a philosophy of law for a period when state-enforced law "pervades" the life of nations to a degree incomparably greater than during the period of Bentham, Austin, Mill, Ihering, Jellinek, and their colleagues. It is a period when the norms of international law and morality are becoming more and more multifarious, permeating deeper and deeper into everyday life. It is a philosophy of law for a period when states of various political and social structures coexist on this globe and cooperate with one another despite their basic differences and antagonisms, and it supplies instruments for cooperation.

The last but not the least aspect of the philosophy of rhetorical positivism is that it is a theory of the period when more and more educated jurists realize that legal norms do not constitute a solid body and are not a fluid in a jar either; they do not have a fixed consistency, but are being "expounded," are something "living," and can be enriched or impoverished by new requirements of life.

CHAPTER IX

Perelman's Achievement Beyond Traditional Philosophy and Politics

1. BETWEEN PROGRESSIVISM AND CONSERVATISM

Professor Chaim Perelman was interviewed by the Polish journalist and scholar, Dr. Wiktor Osiatynski[1] in the summer of 1973 on the occasion of the International Philosophical Congress held in Varna, Bulgaria. The interview was published soon afterwards in the Polish-language weekly, *Kultura*. It never was publicized in the west. In this conversation, whose main topic was equality and justice, Perelman formulated some of his ideas concerning social values and their relationship to politics and reform. Here he articulated his ideas on these topics more clearly than they had been set forth in any of his writings. Apparently, in private conversations with friends he expressed his social and political ideas more succinctly than he did in his written texts prepared for formal purposes.

At the beginning of his interview, Perelman reiterated his already well-publicized idea that equality and justice are values which must be interpreted and clarified as well as creatively pursued in practical life. There is therefore an intrinsic link between philosophy and politics, although, for theoretical and philosophical reasons, Perelman refrained from emphasizing the importance of politics as Jean-Paul Sartre did.

According to Perelman, the question of equality has existed since time immemorial. But it became a truly popular, important subject of philosophical discussion in the eighteenth century. Since the days of the socialist and bourgeois revolutions, it has never ceased to be topical. Whether equality or inequality serves society better, Perelman could not and would not wish to answer. Why? Because the very question is too general and encompasses too many unclear and controversial elements that cannot persuasively or reasonably be answered. Consequently, Perelman responded with his own questions:

---

[1] The quotations in this essay are translated from the manuscript which Dr. Wiktor Osiatynski kindly made available to me. He intends to publish the full text of the conversations with Perelman in his new book. I wish to thank him for the permission to quote his work.

Why do you think that the equal treatment of people is better than unequal treatment? Do you think your answer applies in all circumstances? Which is more important, equal treatment or equal effects? The liberal concept of equality may be narrowed down to equality before the law. Does this mean that we should treat the criminal and the victim in the same equal way under all circumstances? In my opinion, the best and most one could conclude is that one should not treat people unequally without important reasons.

Perelman reached his conclusions in his own way, following the well-known argument that sometimes "compensatory" favorable treatment should be given those who had been treated unfairly by life, to the poor and the physically or socially handicapped. In order to be practical, this reasoning led him to declare that thought about equality must be supplemented by profound reflections on justice.

On the other hand, Perelman argued that one should take the existing reality including the existing legal system as one's point of departure. On the basis of reasoned assessment of reality one should either seek reforms and make changes or leave the situation alone, because order and certainty also represent important social values.

At this point, the interlocutor, Dr. Osiatynski remarked that Dr. Perelman at times speaks as if he were a socialist and at other times as if he were a conservative; does he intend to remain a "pure" philosopher with "clean hands"? Perelman characteristically gave no direct answer to any of these inquiries, but in subsequent argumentation he presented enough material to outline his political philosophy and his reply to the bluntly posed questions.

The following statements by Perelman throw additional light on his reasoning and personality:

> The question of equality emerges in certain circumstances only. When the minimal needs of the people cannot be met the question does not exist. Neither does the problem of equality exist when there is such abundance that everyone is able to procure all they wish, for instance, there is no question, for the time being at least, concerning equal distribution of air. Equality becomes an important and urgent problem when enough goods are at hand to assure a minimum but not enough to meet all the needs . . . It is this minimum which should be assured, and which stimulates our feelings of equality, not the maximum. Today, however, even more and more than the idea of equality, the idea of special privilege and unequal treatment has become more and more urgent and widespread. For instance, more and more people feel that society should accord special favorable treatment to those who are born handicapped – socially or physically. The same reasoning may be applied to underdeveloped countries. Many social and national groups ask for special privileges in order to overcome historical inequalities.

Perelman argued further that the controversies and antagonisms are not the direct result of the perception of inequality itself; the problem, according to him, which is of far greater importance, is the social tension and the "necessity to avoid vast and acute social strains".

His social and political credo, to the best of my knowledge, has never been so clearly or forcefully articulated in any of his other works as it was here:

> The minimum degree of equality a society requires is that the least favored people should not be so desperate as to rebel; on the other hand there should be at least enough inequality so that those who are more competent, more industrious, and gifted should not feel exploited. We know from historical experience that when everyone is always treated equally, the society starts to degenerate. Those who are more intelligent and active prefer to join societies where they will be better rewarded.
>
> The most difficult problem is to maintain a balance between equality and inequality, between social harmony and enterprise. That is the most essential question of practical politics. The same, by the way, can be observed about all other competing social values – a balance between them must be preserved.

At this point the interviewer interjected: "Then what is the most precious, important social value?" Perelman answered:

> In every society, the most important value is the value which is lacking. If the people feel they do not have freedom of speech, then this value becomes paramount. When they are burdened with exploitations, then the most important value is freedom from exploitation. That which they lack begets social tensions. There are no general laws to determine the sources of tensions, rebellions, and methods of coping with them. Society can be regarded as satisfied when people do not complain about their basic minimal needs being satisfied.

The interviewer immediately asked Perelman to clarify whether according to him the most important universal value to which all others are subordinate is "social harmony or such a minimalization of discontent and tension which could also be called 'social agreement'?" Could this specific "minimalism" be further explained? Is it "minimalism" at all? Perelman once more responded in a general way. He did not dispel the interviewer's suspicions but added some qualifications; such a value as "social harmony" or "minimalization of discontent" or similar values are so general that they must be made concrete. Their realization depends not only on the inner force of abstract principles or so called objective situations, but is "determined also by public opinion, public consciousness, and the subjective needs of given society".

This interview of Perelman, largely unnoticed, provides an exceptionally important key to understanding the philosophical and political attitudes of the author. The traditional, although simplistic, question usually asked by every contemporary journalist, author, or scholar, is irrelevant in this case: is he conservative? liberal? socialistic? progressive? democratic? All Perelman's answers and those found in the body of his writings indicate that he regards simple answers to be misleading because his philosophy is beyond these categories, it is *au delá de philosophie traditionelle*; nevertheless, if one may use the famous expression of Geny and Saleilles, he reaches his conclusions *par la philosophie traditionelle*.

Most important is the social content. Perelman does not want to accept uncritically the existing situation in western countries but he disagrees with those who state that socialism and communism were the only alternatives to parliamentary democracy. He does not believe in utopias. He does not believe in any kingdom of complete equality and happiness, he rejects any ideas of sacrifices for unattainable ends, for unreasonable dreams. He insists that methods which can humanize existing situations in our world are most important without specifying what the goals or results should be. He very consistently rejects any theology or earthly or heavenly salvation, any monism, any absolutistic interpretations of human needs and forms of freedom. No form of teleology is acceptable to him. In this frame of mind he developed his theory of argumentation which at the same time is a methodology and a theory.

One can of course argue that the New Rhetoric is chiefly a method of argumentation, merely a method for finding reasonable solutions in the field of politics, law and morality: one can argue that it is not a philosophy or social theory at all because they presuppose the existence of certain values and goals. However, in our time, once such values as human rights, respect for legality, freedom from hunger and religious oppression, are uncontestable human values acknowledged even by international and municipal law, then we must agree that the situation has changed dramatically. Today the problem is how to preserve, secure, and enhance these values in our world which is so badly divided and endangered by various forms of existing and creeping totalitarianism. It is for this reason that Perelman's new theory of argumentation is a new methodology, a new social philosophy and a critical instrument for social reform. One should not, therefore, regard his answers to traditional questions whether he is a conservative or socialist or both at the same time, as evasive. One should simply regard his new theory of argumentation as the appropriate way to find reasonable solutions during a period of decline and transformation of all existing social and political systems and institutions in the west and east.

Let us emphasize that the ideas which Chaim Perelman shared with Dr. Wiktor Osiatynski were not entirely unknown to his closest friends and collaborators. However, we never had an opportunity to interview him systematically and his far-reaching remarks were not recorded by any of us. I had been privileged to have long conversations and exchanges with him from the fifties on and especially during the last years before his death, which were most important to me in my own re-evaluation of my experience, my personal philosophy, and reassessment of the published record of my writings in both the east and the west. The rhetorical approach devised by Perelman became decisive for me. We endlessly discussed to what extent the New Rhetoric might be used by sinister, "reactionary," social forces.

Our conclusions were that of course every philosophy or methodology (and theology) can be applied in defiance of the intentions and wishes of its authors. "Love thy neighbor," after all, was used to sanction the burning at the stake of hapless heretics on the ground that fire cleanses from sin and assures entry to paradise; eternal happiness, it was argued, was more valuable than life on earth. Consequently, an executioner was to be looked upon as the true friend of his victim. Even dialectics, the most revolutionary philosophical method, was employed by Hegel as a defense of the Prussian monarchy. Although the Hegelian subterfuge worked only for a short time, it was fruitful even if its success was brief. Could the New Rhetoric be used for antidemocratic purposes by skillful demagogues? Yes, of course. Nevertheless, the value of a method should not be determined by right how it be abused by perverts and mischief-makers, but on the basis of its genuine meaning, intent, and the results it generally achieves. The possibilities for antidemocratic and unreasonable use of the New Rhetoric are rather limited. I have been convinced that the very concept of audience and dialogue, the process of questioning all premises and challenging all purported facts, precludes bad results. One might go so far as to say the Perelman's theory of argumentation must give nightmares to those who persist in dogmatism, orthodoxy, and tyranny. In order to substantiate this thesis, the origin of The New Rhetoric and its influence should be examined. Its impact on modern political, moral, and juridical philosophy must be weighed.

2. PERELMAN'S GOALS: TO DEFEND REASON AND TOLERANCE

Chaim Perelman was a product of European humanism. He read all the chief scholarly and literary works in their original languages. He was acquainted with the great achievements of human ingenuity in the west and in the east. He was a freethinker, deeply rooted in the Judeo-Christian and secular humanistic ideals of moral responsibility.

He was a formidable debater and a most amiable and loyal personality, always going out of his way to help his friends and colleagues. He was one of the greatest contemporary historians of ideas, but he used his vast knowledge not so much to interpret the past as to apply it as the basis for his own creativity.

Perelman was a Belgian, a Jew, a Pole and an authentic cosmopolitan in the original Stoic meaning of this word. His beliefs were based on deeply ingrained traditional ideals filtered through his critical judgment.

Perelman, although born in Poland, moved to Belgium as a young man. He finished his studies there in the field of law, philosophy, and logic. In the 1930's he returned to Poland in order to learn firsthand about the achievements of the then famous Polish school of logic, mathematics, and positivist philosophy. This school – alongside the Viennese philosophical circle – was also a bastion of liberal, rationalistic, and progressive thought in Poland, then subject to a military dictatorship and the rising influence of fascism. Perelman's respect for and friendship with Professor Tadeusz Kotarbinski, the symbol of Polish open mindedness, secular thought, and tolerance is noteworthy and significant.

During the Nazi occupation, Perelman was active in the Belgian resistance and while in hiding, lacking any access to libraries, wrote his great essay *On Justice* (so far translated into seven languages). His ability to concentrate upon and produce a study on such an abstract and lofty ideal during the darkest days of European and his own personal life, filled with horror, throws a meaningful light on the author. It is significant and symbolic in itself.

After World War II, Perelman assumed the first name, Chaim, as an outward sign of his national and moral feelings and his solidarity with the nation which the Nazis tried to extinguish while the world remained silent. He thought that his dramatic gesture was necessary because he was known as an atheist and an "assimilated cosmopolitan." Without ceasing to be a universalistic scholar and a Belgian, he thought it was proper to accentuate his Jewishness at a time when the Nazi heritage was still alive and sinister forces were seeking to isolate Israel from the world community.[2] Perelman used to demonstrate the close affinity between the new Jewish nation and western culture, between his writings and the spirit of our western civilization.

As we know, there are many Christian theologians who after World War II (concurring with Pope Pius XI) asserted that in order to be a true Christian it is first necessary to be a good Jew. This idea has been brilliantly argued by Professor Hans Kueng. Cardinal Lustiger of Paris announced that he remained a Jew although he interpreted the Holy Scriptures in a different way from that of his ancestors. Perelman, however, seemed to indicate that no one can be a consistent freethinker and a truly enlightened cosmopolitan member of the human race without having a thorough appreciation of the Jewish heritage. He was a true descendent of Spinoza, a Jew who belonged to no temple. He did not believe in creation, the flood, or the miracles on Mount Sinai, but he had close ties to Israel and lectured in Jerusalem about every year, particularly during his last years. He abhorred the intolerance displayed by religious orthodoxy, but the spirit of the Commandments remained deeply ingrained in his soul.

Perelman was uniquely able to combine his nationality and his humanity in his writings. He was an ardent Belgian patriot; he fought in the Belgian underground and participated in Belgian society.

He preserved close ties with Polish scholars and Polish culture at the same

---

[2]   When King Baudouin of Belgium conferred the title of "Baron" on Perelman, he requested the artist to engrave the Menorah on his coat of arms. It is noteworthy that Perelman sought to engage Palestinians in open, public debates with him. They usually refused.

time. From his early school years Perelman was able to distinguish two currents
in Polish history. The first and the most important is the heritage of Polish
open-mindedness and tolerance; he never forgot that in the middle ages, when
the Jews were being massacred all over Europe they found a haven of peace
and hospitality under the dynasties of the Piasts, the Jagiellons, and their
successors.

There was also in Poland another trend, of course, anti-Semitism, which
was reinforced or had been imported from Germany or Russia especially in
the twentieth century.

Between 1918 and 1939, independent Poland was a backward, undemoc-
ratic state. At the same time, however, it was a country where many
nationalities lived together and where creative liberal thought and art thrived.
The strange and unbalanced conditions there, nevertheless, were a source of
inspiration for the Poles and for the Jews. Their love-hate affair was at once
stimulating and numbing.

This gifted Belgian, influenced by this atmosphere, was predestined to create
something innovative. Perelman's New Rhetoric and his New Rationalism
represent a convergence of various cultures and contradictions. He was able
to transform all the disadvantages of his origin and background to powerful
advantage and to a source of inspiration.

3. TOWARD NEW RATIONALISM

Perelman started his campaign in defense of rationalism and reasonableness
at an opportune time. He began his creative scholarly activity when fascist
fanaticism, irrationalism, and military conquests were endangering all of
Europe; on the other hand, the communist regime in the U.S.S.R. had already
lost its revolutionary impetus. Its ideology has ossified into an expanding
set of dogmas, its political structure had become a bureaucratic hierarchy
with its own liturgy, intellectual and physical terror, ritualistic excommuni-
cations, and extirpation of heretics.

We live in a strange period when logic is used for unreasonable and
antidemocratic political purposes. The old much discredited Manichaeism
was forcefully reinvigorated and reintroduced into political and ideological
thinking, at first by the extreme "right" and "left" and soon afterwards it
became a mental disease contaminating the west. This self-serving oversim-
plicity, in the interpretation of the contradictions between "good" and "evil,"
is even infecting many well-educated minds.

At the same time, in the western democracies, "La trahison des clercs"
advanced. The intellectuals and the middle class, broadly interpreted, betrayed
their heritage. The spirit of servility and accommodation and of disinclina-
tion to criticize crept into all areas of social life. Erich Fromm described it
pithily: freedom is becoming burdensome, more and more people in modern
industrial societies seek to escape it. And, let us add, more and more people

find out that freedom in the traditional European meaning, the power of self-determination, may be traded for economic comfort and security. The price did not seem exorbitant: acceptance of degradation into partial mindlessness and moral numbness.

Positivistic moral philosophy, so popular at this time, seemed adequate; since there is no rational basis for moral norms and duties, everyone has the right to determine what is good or bad for himself. Philosophical positivism, which made its debut with the highest scientific aspirations, negated itself, becoming a philosophy of rationalistically logically "justified irrationalism" in morality.

Therefore the campaign of Chaim Perelman to prove that there is and must be a philosophical reasonable link between *sein* and *sollen*, between existence and moral duties, became the most important intellectual and political initiative in the era of the decline, the *"Untergang,"* of the west. If his achievements in this respect are still underestimated, or ignored outright, if not deliberately rejected, especially among western-hemisphere intellectuals, that only shows that – as Hegel observed – the owl of Minerva spreads its wings at dusk. Humanity usually starts to accept the dawn of a new era and the passing of the old one when the downfall of the old order is already near. Even worse, in a period of decline, in the opinion of the shortsighted privileged, those who have reached the lowest points seem to be most advanced.

There is not a more important and urgent task for western intellectuals, statesmen, and teachers than to restore the role of reason to its full brightness and splendor. Today this task is even more complicated than it ever was before.

The domination of the mass media of communications is inseparably connected with the rule of slogans. Appealing platitudes induce people to accept senseless assertions as obvious truths or common-sense directives. This rule of spiritual shallowness adds specific features to prevailing conservative attitudes.

Modern conservatism – be it autocratic, communist, "liberal", or "democratic" – pretends that it is based on principles of reason and common sense in all spheres and at all levels of life. Therefore, analysis of the concept of the kingdom of "Reason" or "Common Sense," and of their real contents, is most necessary in order to defend them against canny, *hinterlistige* (Hegel's expression), treacherous and imperceptible distortions. The new irrationalism puts on a mask of rationalization. This ideologico-intellectual grotesque neither emerged nor could have existed in any previous century.

One can apply to modern platitudes and their pretense to represent wisdom and traditional values, the famous observation of Justice Oliver Wendell Holmes about the false pretenses of natural law adherents. "The believers in natural law seem to accept that what has been familiar to them and their neighbors must be accepted by all humanity."[3]

---

[3]   Oliver Wendell Holmes, *Collected Legal Papers* (New York: Peter Smith, 1952), p. 312.

This remark of Holmes is like Hegel's observation that common sense in the hands of its misinterpreters "holds fast to the evidence of the *senses* and to customary ideas"[4] and expressions. Mindful of the above analyses the New Rhetoric draws conclusions from the fact that what one "sees clearly and distinctly" may not be as clear as it seems. In these social and intellectual circumstances, the very emergence of a new rationalism adjusted to new conditions was an act of liberation, a progressive rebellion, and a cry for reform.

The rhetorical explanation of the fallacies of common sense (or "natural," or "human," "ordinary" reason) caused either by oversimplification or deliberate abuses, has the same point of departure as dialectics. Empirical observations (they always appeal to civilized people) are combined with simplistic widespread beliefs in a given society. These resulting opinions, sentiments, and convictions have been historically formed. They were inherited uncritically from previous generations; they enjoy undeserved credence which is strengthened by the power and respect for tradition, by the appearance of self-evidence, and by a supposed Cartesian clarity and distinctness. The combination of superficial sense observations with traditional opinions form a firm foundation on which simplistic beliefs solidify into well entrenched prejudices and myths, into filters on "uneven mirrors" (Bacon) distorting all messages.

The rhetorical criticism of the peculiar human mental inclination to be misled acknowledges the wisdom of the founder of the dialectical method. Heraclitus argued that "nature loves to hide," it does not easily reveal its secrets. On the contrary, nature likes to deceive its observers when they carelessly either forget that "eyes and ears are bad witnesses for men", or they are too suspicious and fully mistrust their senses; then they hear "like a deaf man," "though present they are not there" and make fools of themselves. Superficial observers do not think about things they experience, they do not understand what they learn, however, they think that they know (Fragment No).[5]

Hegel expressed the same ideas in a simple sentence: " . . . was *bekannt ist, ist darum noch nicht erkannt*" (what is known is not necessarily understood). This is the traditional dialectical approach and with Hegel it reached its zenith. From this point on, the dialectical method had to be developed and updated. Here Perelman entered with his concept of reasonableness and his rationalistic recommendations of the New Rhetoric. Thus he started his trip beyond traditional philosophy.

The creative revival of Aristotelian rhetoric is Perelman's most important and comprehensive achievement. As we have already stated, he could not accept that there can be no reasonable argumentation in the sphere of morality

---

    [4]   G. W. Hegel. 'The Science of Logic', in *Collected Works* (Berlin: 1833), p. 12.
    [5]   Heraclitus, "Fragments," in Milton C. Nahm, *Selections from early Greek Philosophy* (New York: Appleton-Century Crofts, 1964), pp. 71–5.

and public policy. While analyzing world experience, the course and the results of the totalitarian reigns and the aftermath of World War II, the atrocities committed in the name of the ideologies based either on open irrationalism and fanaticism or rationalization of cruelty, he found himself deeply dissatisfied with the prevalent state of scholarship in the field of politics and ethics. Filled with doubt he began, as we have pointed out, to ask the old questions: is it possible that some ideas and decisions can be logical but not reasonable? If something is rational, must it be humane? If there are dictates of reason which are not morally, humanely, commendable, should not the predicaments of our reasoning be critically reassessed? Is it not strange to assert that any normative system is arbitrary and logically indeterminate?

Thus he decided to develop "a logic of value judgments" in order to reject "irrational choices based on interest, passion, prejudice, and myth?[6]

And he stressed repeatedly that this problem was not purely intellectual and logical, but that it has a great topical political impact as well:

Recent history has shown abundantly the sad excess to which such an *attitude* (i.e., *irrational* – emphasis added) can lead.[7]

Perelman had to go beyond traditional theory and methodology because of the practical and theoretical needs of the second half of our century. Traditional empiricism, positivism, rationalism, all their old forms and their current re-editions, were unable to meet new demands in the age of genocide and various forms of totalitarianism.

The New Rhetoric substantiates the traditional values and at times simply restates the obvious requirements of reason and decency. It is desirable, because, as George Orwell – already quoted – wrote in our era the simple restatement of the obvious is unfortunately becoming the first duty of an intelligent man.

4. TOWARD A NEW HUMANISM

My latest two books, *Juridical Positivism and Human Rights* (1981) and *Freedom and Tolerance* (1984) were written under the direct influence of the philosophy and methodology of the New Rhetoric. The new rhetoric is an instrument that is indispensable for the elaboration of a theory of law which is adapted to modern social and political needs. The philosophy of law which, in *Juridical Positivism and Human Rights* is called "positivist realism," is an amalgam of traditional juridical European positivism and American jurisprudence, internal and municipal norms of human rights, and the philosophy

---

[6] Chaim Perelman, 'The New Rhetoric. A Theory of Practical Reasoning' in *The Great Ideas Today* (Chicago: Encyclopedia Britannica, 1970). Reprinted in *The New Rhetoric and the Humanities* (Dordrecht, London: Reidel Publishing Co., 1979), p. 8.

[7] *Ibid.*, p. 9.

and methodology of the New Rhetoric. It emerges as a theory of law adjusted to the new realities of the end of the twentieth century. It encompasses the best progressive traditions of the philosophy and practice of law and the experience of many modern societies. It is a theory of law which explains the nature of law and can aid the perennial struggle for a democratic social order and human rights, international cooperation, and sovereignty.

Positivist realism can overcome the recurrent mythology of natural law theories. Indeed, both positivistic and natural law theories survived because of their mutual weaknesses. The criticism of the eighteenth-century version of natural law was followed by the domination of juridical positivism in the nineteenth century. But at the end of this century, natural law theories have enjoyed a revival. The juridical positivists usually underestimated the progressive implications of natural law theories as represented for instance by Locke, Rousseau or their American counterparts but they pointed out that these theories were not scientific, that life was changing too profoundly to assert that there can be any unchangeable rules.

On the other hand, juridical positivism represented a tremendous step forward in the development of the juridical sciences, but its program was too limited. This theory could also be used for government-sponsored terror and legalized illegality.

In my books, this weakness in a narrowly interpreted and even distorted juridical positivism was overcome by combining juridical positivism with the concept of human rights. These theories can be broadened and transformed into a new philosophy by applying the new theory of argumentation. In this way the New Rhetoric would have an important theoretical and practical role as a philosophical foundation of modern progressive jurisprudence and as a necessary instrument to overcome contradictions between the requirements of municipal and international law. It makes the traditional application of the right of Antigone obsolete, but perpetuates the idea of her philosophy and mandates the securing of human rights and political freedom.

Regarding the interpretation and application of law. The New Rhetoric serves as an important instrument for overcoming traditional antagonisms between "subjectivists" and "objectivists," those who want to establish the subjective will of the legislator or the objective sense of the legal norms.

It may be that these controversies will never cease, but thanks to the New Rhetoric which helps to combine American and European experience, the discussions can be fruitful and help the cause of democracy and human rights.

The New Rhetoric also serves as the indispensable philosophical foundation of political pluralism. Once the notion of absolute truths and monism were so effectively undermined, a reasonable rhetorical justification for the co-existence of contradictory values was established. The New Rhetoric rejects absolute relativism in any sphere of life and thought. At the same time, however, it helps to develop concepts which are new and useful, although from the traditional Cartesian point of view may be regarded as heretical. It is possible that two contradictory statements concerning law, politics, and morality, can to a certain extent be justified. In order to find out which represents the best solution, one should apply the method of the wise judge, the hero of Lessing's play, *Nathan the Wise*. Everyone should endeavor to gain esteem, friendship, love and a communion of minds. The final verdict should be reached by our "children's children's children". . . .

In this way the New Rhetoric has become a philosophical foundation for the modern concept of tolerance. It should prevail in all spheres of public and private life.

Like every great discovery in the history of human thought, Perelman's recommendations appear simple and obvious. It seems strange that we had not recognized them earlier. The meaning of the new methodology and philosophy is distinct, although the name be it the New Rhetoric or the New Theory of Argumentation, does not manifest it so directly and clearly; Perelman's is a rationalism not limited to formulas and logical conclusions, it is inseparable from reasonable and humane inferences.

The publication of the New Rhetoric as a new philosophy is another turning point in the endless struggle of reason and enlightenment against old and new, primitive and sophisticated, types of mental and emotional enslavement. Anyone seeking effectively to fight against the Kingdom of Darkness must in one way or another use the methods elaborated by Chaim Perelman. The rhetoric he rediscovered cannot be disregarded without grave consequences for those who strive for progress, humanism, freedom, and tolerance. One can use rhetorical methods and means without mentioning the name of the founder and his accomplishments, but one cannot ignore them altogether. The New Theory of Argumentation is becoming the common property of thoughtful people who try to preserve and enlarge their sphere of freedom, tolerance, and reasonable activity.

CHAPTER X

The New Rhetoric is Modern Humanism

1. NEW PROBLEMS

Our reflections on the New Rhetoric lead us to conclude that the New Rhetoric today has become a tool to develop new forms of humanism; it is humanistic in itself.

"Humanism" and "Humanistic" have many interpretations. The word became popular at the confluence of the Middle Ages and modern times. There is no doubt that humanistic tendencies were known in previous centuries although they were not called like that. Whenever and wherever individuals are oppressed by social structures and political powers, protests must be raised against such oppression. Such protests are the heart of every struggle for a life of dignity and freedom.

There are many forms of oppression and consequently many forms of humanism. Every oppressive action sooner or later calls forth forces favoring progress and humanism. Modern humanism is of course based on previous humanistic movements, struggles, victories, and defeats. Modern societies have invented new forms of spiritual enslavement which are more subtle and sophisticated than any in the past and therefore it is sometimes difficult to detect, criticize, fight and overcome them. The struggle for humanism never ends.

At times it is most important simply to detect the forces inimical to social activism and the development of the human personality. This is the first task of rhetorical methodology in the service of humanism: to establish what went wrong, what are the sources, how can they be prevented?

We know that there are thousands of frequently contradictory definitions of humanism, at times general, at times detailed. On the basis of the experience of the last century we conclude that the most essential features of a humanistic approach to life are: individuals should be given the chance to develop their personal talents and energies; they should be able to be creative and to become happy.

In this respect Pico della Mirandola, one of the founders of modern humanism and the concept of freedom, substantiated the famous biblical phrase that God has created man in his own image. Mirandola argued that God's most important features was creativity, and this gift of nature or God should be regarded as the most precious and the most characteristic for every human being. Continuing the interpretation of certain rabbis and Talmudists, Pico proclaimed the human being as the highest creature, even above the angels who are merely servants to God. Man is almost equal to God, according to God's own will and design; this is the credo of every type of humanism.

It is obvious that all of Pico's theological considerations were indeed secular. He simply used Scripture as a springboard to present the human being as the highest product of creation whose essence and value is creativity and self-determination.

This basic concept of humanism is also a philosophical foundation of the New Rhetoric. Once the New Rhetoric took as its basic proposition that nothing is absolutely good or sacred except human dignity, one must constantly search for higher values, for better forms and ways of life. There are three specific areas that are especially important for modern humanism: social and individual justice, freedom from oppression with a genuine opportunity for a decent life, and tolerance and privacy.

2. SOCIAL AND INDIVIDUAL JUSTICE

The concept of justice resulted from experience which was perceived as unjust. Justice pertains to the relations of individuals and society. All the problems of justice concerning the situation of an individual must be interpreted from the broader concept of social conduct, activity and ideas. There is no need to repeat Plato's reasoning who, while using Socrates as his alter ego, proved that even lying and stealing may be considered just acts when the intention was good for the country or for one's friends who were in distress (deceiving a friend by calling liquids served him "wine" instead of medicine).

From hundreds of treatises concerning justice, Perelman was able to distill a formal definition of justice according to which, "just is when you treat another in the same way as you would all other representatives of the same class of people." Perelman convincingly proved that the gist of the problem is to apply generalities to real social groups, individuals, and even nations.

There is no doubt in civilized countries that all persons should be equal before the law and should have a chance to improve their standard of living and social position. But what are the criteria that define a better social position or a higher standard of living? And what does it mean to have a fair chance to achieve something better and higher? Some are convinced that to give a chance should also include a push to take a positive step forward, should include real help to achieve something new. This means that those who are disadvantaged, from the economic or racial point of view, should be given certain privileges in order to help overcome their disadvantages and advance them to higher levels. Therefore, in Communist countries the governments tried to recruit the children of poor peasants and workers for special courses which could assure them admission to the universities, although their preparation has been inferior. We know that in the U.S. these questions are being partially solved with the institution of "affirmative action". This solution is highly controversial socially and politically. From the rhetorical point of view any form of "affirmative action" represents a so-called "confused idea," which may be interpreted in various ways. Beneficial, or at times detrimental. It is certain, however, that the problem of how to give active help exists. It is not easily resolved and it can not be put aside, just like that.

Even more complicated are the questions of justice when we consider relations between privileged and underprivileged nations or continents. The countries of the Third World are convinced that they deserve special benefits from the countries that enjoy a higher standard of living. The first response of the nations who live better is that their standards of living are not very high, that they cannot even solve the question of their own underprivileged in their own countries. Surplus resources, if any, are meager and it is impossible to meet the expectations of others.

It seems that since our globe, as is said, has shrunk, we have acquired more problems regarding justice than we had in previous generations when nations, countries, and continents were isolated. We even must discuss whether the livable space has been inherited by us from the previous generation or whether it is simply held in trust by us for future generations. Today more than ever, the questions of justice are global. Is it just to waste air and water resources which are regarded the common property of humanity? If it is a common property, what restrictions may justifiably be put to on the use of natural resources by nations, social groups, and individuals? All these questions are extremely complicated and can be solved only partially and only temporarily. We can never find a permanent truly just solution, but we must openly discuss these questions and argue all the pros and cons. We must realize that we will be required repeatedly to return to the starting point of every discussion and re-argue what had been previously determined.

From the point of view of justice, global, continental, and national problems present new forms of the eternal question: the actions of the individual and his treating others as he would have them treat him, now that the world has become a "global village." If the golden rule or Kant's Imperatives are the most generally accepted precepts concerning individual justice, then Perelman's question re-emerges: how can the general be translated into the concrete and individual?

Problems of individual justice are not isolated, they pertain to relationships between individuals and society. The two are usually intertwined.

Relations between individuals are regulated by custom, morality and law. Of course, individuals will ask for more than legally is their due according to the rules of morality and decency. Sometimes one gives up a legal entitlement because for moral reasons it would be improper to insist on receiving it. These reflections show that even in the areas that are relatively well-regulated by legal and moral norms concerning individuals there are many exceptional situations and then one must consider these relationships, taking into account general concepts and problems of justice. But these concepts, as we know, are so general that any indication must be analyzed in a creative way. Even those trained in law, philosophy and theories of justice will disagree. It seems, therefore, that even relationships between individuals must be subjected to humanistic scrutiny in which rhetorical argumentation will be helpful.

We know that in every civilized country the principle of equality before the law cannot easily and automatically be realized. In contemporary society even a simple case involving a customer and vendor may depend on the financial power of the adversaries. From the formal, legal, point of view the adversaries are equal. But, indeed, an element of injustice is introduced when one of the adversaries cannot afford to hire a good lawyer, or cannot afford to pay for a protracted proceeding. In 1991 there was a case in the U.S. which caused public outrage. It reached the U.S. Supreme Court. An attorney for a defendant who was sentenced to death appealed for a retrial on the basis of *habeas corpus*. The appeal was rejected because the defendant had missed, by one day, the deadline for an earlier appeal to a state court because, as he explained, he had no money to pay the fees and to hire an attorney. The U.S. Supreme Court decided that once the earlier state deadline had been missed, it would not intervene to delay the execution.

From the humanistic and humanitarian point of view, the decision was outrageous. The whole spirit of the New Rhetoric and examples which could be regarded as similar analyzed by Perelman himself, show that in order to realize justice and humanism one should take into account the highest values, the protection of life and the protection of the innocent who might become victims of judicial error. If there could be a fraction of doubt, it should choose protection of life and innocence.

The New Rhetoric is especially disposed towards developing arguments which can help to defend and protect individuals against injustices. These can be caused by an imperfect system of social, political, and legal institutions and by the fact that those who are entitled to enforce justice are only human beings themselves who inherently are imperfect.

3. FREEDOM FROM OPPRESSION: FREEDOM TO CHOOSE AND CREATE

Among the many aspects of freedom, freedom *from* oppression and persecution is supreme. Historically this attitude may be justified. First of all, freedom must be defined in a *negative* way, as freedom from arbitrary and capricious decisions by authorities, and only afterward in a positive way, as freedom *for* creative activity.

Modern humanists chiefly stress that man will be free if he overthrows the tyranny of a despotic government and becomes independent of the oppressive domination of various rulers and autocrats. The emergence of constitutional government and parliamentary rule was therefore a decisive step in the development of the idea of freedom and of genuine individual freedom. Soon, however, it was found that the results of that revolutionary achievement were limited.

The American and French Constitutions and the respective declarations on the rights of the citizen and "natural" freedoms of the people are classic expressions of the development of the idea of freedom. They are directed against governmental oppression. They are highly revered and justly so. Although we have entered into a new stage of the evolution of the idea of freedom it still is necessary to protect these freedoms from invasions. At times, under the guise of protecting freedom and promoting the interests of the people, governments have instituted laws inimical to the principles of freedom. One should not forget that right and left wing totalitarianisms can develop under relatively liberal and free societies.

After the defeat of fascist totalitarianism during World War II, and after the collapse of such fascist states as the Spanish and Portuguese regimes (Franco and Salazar), the collapse of many communist totalitarian governments followed. Nevertheless, the bacillus of totalitarianism has not been eradicated and many social and political causes have fostered its rebirth.

Therefore, the struggle for freedom as expressed in the constitutions of all western countries and in the declarations and documents of the United Nations must continue. This campaign must take into account new political situations and environments.

The famous Hegelian statement that freedom is "comprehended necessity" has entered a new phase in the Western understanding of freedom. There are many avenues for interpreting the Hegelian statement either in the spirit of conservatism, reformism, or revolution. The Hegelian idea that whatever is real must be necessary and whatever is necessary must be real, was interpreted by the Prussian loyalists as a glorification of the existing monarch. It became clear in a short time, however, that truly necessary and real is only what is reasonable; on the other hand, what is unreasonable, like an obsolete regime, must be changed and only after such a change will the balance between freedom and reasonableness, necessity and reality be restored.

According to the dialectical philosophy of Hegel when what is real is not reasonable and necessary, it merely appears to be what it is. Indeed whatever is obsolete must be forcibly overthrown, if need be, by the devotees of freedom. Consequently, a transformation of the concept of freedom took place in the second half of the nineteenth century and almost became prevalent in the twentieth. According to the new concept it is not sufficient to proclaim in the constitutions that people are free and equal. They must be given the opportunity to develop their talents and vital forces.

The new ideas of freedom were developed by many political philosophers, some seemingly contradictory and controversial. The philosophies of socialism, neo-liberalism (some types only), the welfare state, Catholic social doctrine and the American ideas of the New Deal and the Great Society emphasized the activity which governments must undertake to give the people a real chance to develop, to enhance their personal power and freedom, to assure justice in society. According to this new concept, the mere right to criticize the government cannot by itself be sufficient. In order to secure freedom and justice, society has more duties than simply securing privacy and individual freedom of speech. It must create conditions in which all citizens can get the education they need, including secondary and even higher education. They must be free from poverty and degrading social conditions; man's primary economic and cultural requirements need to be met in order to assure equal opportunity.

In connection with our considerations of the new moral norms and the requirements of happiness, prevailing humanistic opinion requires that governments supply their citizens with means which can help them to develop their personal talents.

Perelman made it clear in his writings that he adhered to the second, modern concept of freedom. He used to stress that freedom consists in the power to overcome difficulties and obstacles on the road to achieving one's desires and purposes. He also asserted, without using Hegelian terminology, that freedom is inseparable from understanding that only reasonable desires can be fulfilled. In this way, the New Rhetoric was meant by its founder to establish what is reasonable, what should be pursued to achieve it and to satisfy the pursuers of individual and national purposes.

We can therefore regard the New Theory of Argumentation as an instrument helping to understand reality better and to adjust reality to the modern meaning of freedom and justice.

4. TOLERANCE AND PRIVACY

The essence and basis of the New Rhetoric is tolerance. Its method can be developed and applied only in an atmosphere of tolerance. It is also the means to struggle for tolerance. But once tolerance becomes a way of life – even if limited – the further development of democracy and freedom depends on the proper application of the rhetorical method in daily life.

One of the greatest spiritual fathers of the methodology of the New Rhetoric was Benedict Spinoza. The condemnation of his religious view and his expulsion from the Jewish religious community, with the tacit and informal approval of the Christian dogmatists, was a memorable lesson from which Spinoza drew all the appropriate conclusions. In his writings he set forth the basic and classic arguments in favor of tolerance.

Spinoza's ultimate conclusion can be presented as follows: freedom of thought and speech is inseparable from freedom of assembly. If the people are forbidden to speak their thoughts, they will be afraid even to think and that would be a loss for all humanity. Freedom of speech and even freedom of thought are useless if people are not free to assemble to exchange their thoughts. It is futile to forbid people to assemble for social and political reasons because they will do so surreptitiously anyway. Laws which interfere with these three inseparable freedoms must be abhorred and disregarded by the citizens. When such laws are rejected and disobeyed, the whole political structure is undermined, the citizenry becomes alienated from its usurping government and the necessary link of trust between the citizens and the authorities is ruptured.

Spinoza may have been the first thinker to have said that freedom of thought, speech and assembly are inseparable. He was the first to explain the links between these freedoms (including freedom of religion, as one of them). Indeed, he invented what we call the chain of freedoms today. The rupture of one of its links today destroys the entire chain, a government which curtails such liberties undermines its own existence. The recent downfall of both right-and-left-wing authoritarian governments is the best proof of how correct Spinoza was when he wrote his observations more than three centuries ago.

Spinoza could of course not know that such an intolerant government would undermine not only its political existence and its moral legitimacy, but also thwart the development of the economic forces of its people. The downfall of the Soviet political and economic system, often referred to as "real socialism," proved that the demoralization caused by despotism and intolerance chokes off other development as well.

Spinoza's observations are deeper and further reaching than the famous opinion of Lord Acton: every power corrupts, absolute power corrupts absolutely. Spinoza understood that not only the rulers but the subjects as well are demoralized by power. And finally he concluded that a government which deprives its citizens of their liberties, which persecutes those who think freely and independently, endangers the welfare and peace not only of its own people but of its neighbors as well. One could conclude that Spinoza agreed that "peace perpetuates peace, freedom reinforces freedom." (Maneli, *Freedom and Tolerance*, op. cit. p. 103)

There is a close relationship between Spinoza's view of tolerance and his philosophy of freedom. His point of departure is the idea that the human being should not be regarded as a cog in a machine. The human being who is autonomous, a value in himself, should be treated as the end and purpose of every social organization and political institution. The hope of future salvation and the requirements of a happy immortality should not restrict his activity and should not dominate his life.

Spinoza also understood the social nature of human beings; his ideal can be expressed simply: cooperation of the people obedient to reason; the association of people should not be subject to accidental impulses, but free people should serve one another following the requirements of reason.

Spinoza's conclusion is also one of the points of departure of the New Rhetoric. To be truly free, people must be reasonable and knowledgeable. There is a link between rationality and freedom, only reasonable people can truly live in harmony with one another. Reason must rule over emotions because those who are dominated by passions are unable to distinguish between good and bad.

"But human liberty is greater, the more man can be guided by reason and moderate his appetite" (Spinoza, *A Political Treatise*, p. 298, The Chief Works of Benedikt Spinoza, Dover Publication., Inc. 1955).

The methodology of the New Rhetoric was also influenced by Spinoza's observation that the people must be well informed about the situation in society and in the state. Governmental secrecy is harmful to social achievements and freedoms:

> So it is supreme folly to wish to transact everything behind the backs of citizens and to expect that they will not judge ill of the same and will not give everything an unfavorable interpretation. For if the populace could moderate itself, and suspend its judgment about the things with which it is imperfectly acquainted or judge rightly of things by the little it knows already, it would surely be more fit to govern than to be governed. (Spinoza, *A Theologico-Political Treatise*, Dover Publication, Inc., 1951, New York, Chapter VII, Section 27).

This is the approach of the New Rhetoric as well. People who are misinformed or uninformed are unable to make correct decisions and, what is even worse for government, they tend to interpret events to the detriment of the secretive governments. According to the New Rhetoric and Spinoza's philosophy of tolerance, there is a close link between knowledge, information, freedom, tolerance, efficient government, and the activities of the governed.

The New Rhetoric also has a spiritual foundation erected in the period of the Enlightenment. In the *Encyclopaedia* edited by Diderot and d'Alembert, under the title "Tolerance," one reads:

> Tolerance in general terms, is the virtue of all feeble beings destined to live with creatures similar to themselves.

This is the point of departure for the philosophy of Enlightenment. People are feeble: they are weaklings condemned to live together in mutual tolerance because otherwise life would be miserable and nasty. The intelligence of man is limited because of lack of knowledge and passions. These human defects can, at least partially, be neutralized by the power of reason and an inclination to mutual respect. Respect for one another is the gist of tolerance.

According to the philosophers of the Enlightenment the principles of tolerance must be explained and propagated by philosophers. They should fight against all kinds of prejudice and fanaticism and in this way inspire people to be open-minded and to practice tolerance in their daily lives. Without tolerance, peace and mutual cooperation, advancement and prosperity will never come.

The New Rhetoric agree with the philosophers of the Enlightenment that there are many sources of discord, contradiction and disagreement. The author of the article on "Tolerance," M. Romilly, wrote that humanity is very fertile at producing conflicts and misunderstandings. But it should be our principle – this is also the opinion of the New Rhetoric – that the more sources there are for differences and disagreements, the more reasons we have to promote mutual respect and tolerance.

The New Rhetoric also accepts another Enlightenment idea. Once we agree that the human mind is an imprecise instrument, that we are unable to reach absolute truth, that what is evident to one mind is obscure to another; once we agree that the proof sufficient for one person is not persuasive to another, we should be tolerant. Otherwise we will never be able to overcome unavoidable deficiencies of the human mind and thinking.

Since the Enlightenment, those who promote tolerance have clearly distinguished between a tolerant attitude and behavior and "culpable indifference." The authors of Encyclopaedia thought that we should distinguish between support for humanity and tolerance for those who err. We differentiate between the indifference or forgiveness for those who hold mistaken ideas and those who proclaim anti-human fanaticism and disregard for freedom. Tolerance cannot extend fully to those who want to destroy it and replace it with crime, persecution, and the rule of the sword instead of the rule of reason. What methods should be used to defend tolerance and a tolerant way of life against its enemies? This is the question. Obviously the answer cannot be the one that was proposed by St. Just during the French Revolution: no freedom for the enemies of freedom.

The New Rhetoric also poses this question. There is no absolutely correct answer. But we are sure that the development of democracy and the culture of society and its involvement in the process of argumentation and counterargumentation can create a climate which will make the return of despotism impossible. Nevertheless, there are no guarantees.

Lastly, the New Rhetoric agrees with Diderot that there is a close link between personal happiness and tolerance. Diderot wrote:

> I wish to be happy: that is the first article of a code that takes precedence over all legislation, over any religious system whatever (Diderot, *Selected Writings*, New York: London: Macmillan Co., 1966, p. 304).

The New Rhetoric agrees that it makes no sense to ask whether a human being has the right to pursue happiness or to be happy, because it is natural for everyone to seek happiness and every government and legislator should remember this precept of nature, reason, and decency. Diderot frequently used to repeat "Let your legislature and morality never forbid innocent pleasure" (*Ibid*).

Diderot and other rationalists and humanists, old and contemporary, seem to apply the medical maxim to morality and politics: "*Primum non nocere*" (First, do no harm). This is one of the most important and self-evident principles of morality and decency. Do not deter people from approaching their own happiness in their own way. Do not forbid achieving it according to their wishes, predilections, and even whims so long as they do not hurt others. Neither society nor governments should interfere with small or great pleasures. Diderot's final recommendation could be expressed in the following way:

> Do not meddle, do not poke into anyone else's business. Do not intrude into your neighbor's soul! Be tolerant! (Maneli, *Freedom and Tolerance, op. cit.*, p. 107).

Renaissance and Enlightenment philosophers believed that reason should restrict all passions and emotions. As they knew very well, however, human beings must be passionate and a person without passion is a monster (Diderot, *Early Philosophical Work*, Chicago-London: The Open Court Publishing Co. (1915), p. 29).

Diderot's observations about what people really are like were taken to heart by the New Rhetoric in its quest for appropriate and reasonable appeals to gain the adherence of different audiences. We are also deeply convinced that happiness and tolerance require that no political power should be placed in the hands of fanatics or ideologues who pretend to know the highest and absolute truths and want to save humanity, whether those to be saved like it or not.

The New Rhetoric also agrees with Diderot and other rationalists and humanists that intolerance does not exist by itself as an autonomous phenomenon; it is always part and parcel of an intolerant political system which cares less for people's well-being but more for abstract, dogmatic principles and the power itself.

Usually dogmatists and especially the clergy propagate fear in order to discourage and frighten their opponents. They insult instead of trying to persuade them because dogmatists usually lack both knowledge and intelligence; when they run short of arguments they take refuge in invective. The Encyclopedists recalled the answer which Menippus gave to Jupiter: "you thunder instead of answering, are you then wrong?"

This is also the conviction of the New Rhetoric. Those short of arguments, insult and thunder. Thus the New Rhetoric agrees with the final recommendation of Diderot concerning dialogue: "*Find arguments.*" (*Ibid.*).

The tradition of justice, freedom, and tolerance discussed above resulted in the legal, moral, and political concept of privacy which ultimately was proclaimed by Justice Brandeis and American jurisprudence in the 20th century.

This American contribution to modern civilization also became one of the most precious assets of modern humanism.

In this way, one more link was created between modern humanism and the New Rhetoric. This is one more reason why we regard the New Rhetoric as an additional philosophical basis for humanism and also a method for the elaboration and justification of *perennial* humanistic social values which are always *new* at the same time.

CHAPTER XI

The New Rhetoric as Philosophy and Methodology

1. BASIC PREMISES

Throughout these pages we have endeavored to highlight the implications of the title of the book which is significant from every point of view. The New Rhetoric is both the philosophy and methodology for the new century. There is always a close relationship and interdependence between a philosophical system and the methodology which its founders used to apply it.

We already mentioned that Perelman had to create and develop his ideas in the thick of a constant struggle against open and indirect covert criticism. He did not live in an ivory tower but had to act, fight and argue. He usually lacked the time and comfort to elaborate his philosophy point by point in a logical sequence the way he truly had wanted to present it.

The requirements of scholarly and social life compelled him to stress the questions which were the most novel and important at any given time and circumstances. Consequently, some of his theses were not fully documented but today they can be elaborated through a philosophical analysis of what he left behind.

Perelman's work is complete in the sense that the founder of the New Rhetoric is no longer among us and will not add to it. We should not, however, try to present his ideas according to our own views, but should consider the body of his contributions as they exist. It is not necessary to recount the stages of his own intellectual development. It is his whole work which should be interpreted correctly and creatively. An account of Perelman's achievements should begin with the most fundamental and difficult question which is his criticism of the positivistic theory of morality. We know that he rejected the idea that morality, politics, and social values and a justification of legal norms should be abandoned to the irrationalists. He clearly stated that this intellectual and moral sell-out was one of the most immediate and important incentives for him to develop his own theory, the New Rhetoric.

He rejected not only the positivistic and pragmatic views of morality and politics, but also the philosophical premises underlying those concepts. Nevertheless, he was unable to join the positivist campaign against metaphysics. He disagreed with positivists like Moritz Schlick, Ludwig Wittgenstein, Rudolf Carnap, Bertrand Russell, and others, but he was on good personal terms with A. J. Ayer while rejecting the principles of his philosophy. Although Ayer himself officially rejected positivism, he nevertheless tacitly adopted its basic propositions. The differences between positivism and Perelman's philosophy, for scholarly reasons, deserve more attention than has yet been given to them in the literature because implicit in them are the foundations of the New Rationalism.

It seems appropriate here to observe that Perelman called Aristotelian rhetoric his main inspiration. In fact, he appropriated another important element from Aristotle's philosophy, his epistemology and his ideas concerning truth. Truth, according to Aristotle, is evident when there is *adaequatio rei et intellectus*. Perelman never doubted that our minds, as Bacon put it, are like mirrors in which the world in which we live is reflected. Perelman also accepted Bacon's metaphor that mirrors are uneven and that consequently reflections therein may be distorted, but only to a certain extent; they are not entirely false but rather are incomplete. Nevertheless, reality exists and its reflection in the human mind takes place and is usually partially correct. In this way, all the positivistic doubts about whether we ever deal with the real world or only with subjective impressions or sensual data were swept aside and rejected by Perelman. The whole problem of Kantian transcendence was also rejected as non-existent. There is no impassable barrier between the world and our minds. He of course agreed that the process of increasing our knowledge is very complicated, sometimes treacherous and staggering with its horrendous possibilities. However, if one takes into account the needs and requirements of practical human activity, the hesitations and doubts of abstract philosophers must be overcome. Both Marxists and pragmatists tried to overcome the positivistic deficiency described above, but it was Perelman who found his own right original solution, in the tradition which was initiated in the west by Democritus and Aristotle.

This brings us to the second premise of Perelman's philosophy. It was not devised – we stressed this already many times – to serve as an instrument for pure reasoning nor as an instrument for discussion alone. Nor is it merely a tool to refute erroneous opinions. It is a device to promote reasonable and rational activity. Consequently, Wittgenstein's reasoning, as presented in his *Tractatus Logico-Philosophicus* (see para. 5.62; 5.64; 6.45) that solipsism might be quite correct and, if applied strictly, would coincide with pure realism, is alien to the spirit and letter of the New Rhetoric. A reasonable, practical, individual would never even flirt with solipsism.

It should be quite clear that Perelman rejected all philosophies which could be called subjective idealism like the reasoning of Hume, which maintained that we deal simply with our subjective experience or subjective sense data. Perelman propounded his theory for intellectual and practical purposes, therefore he regarded sensory information as a means of reflecting the real matter, the world, the society. The problem discussed by Roman Ingarden in his

"*Discourse Whether the World Exists*" was alien to him. He did not doubt the existence of the world and therefore he developed his theory as a tool to investigate natural and social phenomena. It was his own traditional and innovative way to expand human reasonable activity and freedom.

The analysis of Perelman's ontology and epistemology further illuminates why he regarded his essay dedicated to Professor Tadeusz Kotarbinski, who had been his teacher, so important. Kotarbinski was the greatest Polish philosopher to represent rationalism, materialism, liberalism and tolerance in the twentieth century.

Kotarbinski's materialism, strongly criticized in People's Poland, was not communist materialism. Perelman, like Kotarbinski, continued the best European tradition of critical materialism, free of all dogmatic inferences, and free of the absolutistic pretensions of the Soviet version of dialectical materialism.

Perelman constructed his philosophy of values such as freedom, justice, tolerance and equality on those ontological and epistemological foundations. His rejection of the idea that values cannot be justified rationally is based on the historical development of those values and their acceptance by a more and more universal audience. He did not regard perceptions of justice and freedom as solely or entirely individual, solipsistic, and subjective, instead he took into account the interdependence of individual and social activity. Once people communicate they must reach a consensus. The opinion of an audience, can become objective sooner or later and should be treated as such. This is the connection between Perelman's epistemology, ontology, and sociology. These are the reasons why the New Rhetoric should be regarded not simply as a polemical and critical exercise, but as a new, original, positive, yet not positivistic philosophy, epistemology, ontology and sociology.

One of the main purposes of this book is to refute and reject the negative image usually connected with rhetorical argumentation.

The New Rhetoric should not be narrowed down to a method for undermining established beliefs and for shaking up entrenched dogmas. Indeed, the New Rhetoric is basically a method to elaborate new ideas and new concepts of life. Its chief purpose is not to criticize for criticism's sake, but to offer criticism in order to find new solutions to old and new problems.

Mutatis mutandis, the same can be said about the rhetorical theory of the interpretation of law. Legal interpretation is not only for the sake of a critical analysis of juridical norms but should aim toward a novel understanding and new possibilities to apply them to new cases, including cases previously unknown to the legislator and unforeseen by him. Thus it is proper to stress once more that the New Rhetoric is an instrument to achieve practical purposes.

2. NEW SOCIAL AWARENESS

Once we agree that the New Rhetoric is based on the historical achievements of the human spirit, of our culture and civilization, one should take into account a factor which is even more immeasurable and volatile than any other element. It is the question of the critical powers of the human mind, which from the social viewpoint undermine all forms of totalitarianism and "creeping totalitarianism." We often distinguish between "Fascist" and "Communist totalitarianism." Far more significant are the effects of totalitarian ideologies and propaganda in various countries.

Today, as a result of the events of 1989–1992 in communist and post-communist countries, we must note that the communist revolution in spheres of education and culture (let us not confuse it with the so-called "cultural revolution") is bearing fruits unforeseen by "Kremlinologists" and other "specialists" in communism. There were progressive thinkers in Eastern Europe who for many decades understood the deep psychological changes fostered by the compulsory study of history, world literature, and philosophy. Communist indoctrination required these studies. The authorities tried to make selections. But even the selected texts remain texts. Any knowledge of the history of human thought enlightens and stimulates independent thinking even though the purpose of the teacher may be biased, and intended to influence the audience in a way that is useful to the government. The genius of human intelligence cannot be returned into a bottle once it has escaped.

These are the reasons for our conclusion that the Communist system of general and political education prepared its own "gravediggers," as Marx and Engels used to call the proletariat in the capitalist system. In every post-communist country across which the democratic avalanche swept we find thousands of gifted, well-educated people fully capable of thinking independently and acting creatively to achieve their democratic purposes.

The New Rhetoric has to take these facts into account. The facts that in the East and in the West, as well as in the post-colonial countries, there are growing numbers of people who are able to think critically and progressively. They have created a foundation for the rhetorical concept of society which rejects any autocratic, messianic and utopian tendencies. In order to fight for progress and strive for freedom, tolerance and welfare, beliefs in an earthly or heavenly paradise, secular or religious, became evidently superfluous. Humankind has already expanded its knowledge and experience to such an extent that we now can reasonably act on a daily basis and consciously realize our ideals of freedom, self-reliance, social and moral responsibility.

The rhetorical philosophy and methodology is based not so much on the ruins of prior and bankrupt political and social systems and their obsolete ideology and philosophy as it is based on a new social awareness and on the boundless experience which has been distilled for us by our predecessors.

3. RESOLUTIONS FOR THE NEW CENTURY

The events of recent years indicate once more how deep the ideological crisis is in the east as well as in the west. The total collapse of the Communist regimes especially in the Soviet Union illuminates better than any other historical event how unreasonable are attempts to construct a new society, or a new social and political system, according to *a priori* schemes. Any plan for paradise on earth, be it secular or religious, is incompatible with the demands and experience of our daily life and reason.

The New Rhetoric is a philosophy for the new century because we live in a period in which humanity has accumulated more experience than ever before. The fact that we have so much data concerning various forms of government, Communist and capitalist, welfare states and systems of unregulated market forces, colonialism and decolonization, various phases of democratization and totalitarianism, enables us to draw necessary conclusions on how to act in a progressive and reasonable way.

Every social and political system that has existed during our century has provided certain advantages for the public but has, at the same time, denied others. We have so much experience now that at times we might we might be inclined to repeat after Aldous Huxley, "Time must stop." But time cannot stop and we must adopt new methods and develop new forms of social organization.

The New Rhetoric supplies the methodology which can serve us at this stage. Once we agree that no institution or method is perfect, we must be open to experimentation and new ideas, and try to apply them. We must, at the same time, observe and analyze all that is happening around us, determine what is advantageous, continue what seems good, or start all over again taking into account newly acquired disappointments and experience.

These continuous ups and downs may cause much pain. Whenever we begin with new social institutions and forms of life we must be aware that there are no specialists able to make our arrangements work smoothly. The latest examples indicate how much creative imagination is required when on the ruins of the socialist economic system a new one must be built based on private property and competition. Those who know the principles of market economy are only familiar with the western situation and cannot know all the interconnections and details that exist in a country which communism has bankrupted in so many ways.

The New Rhetoric is a methodology and philosophy which can help ease the transition from one economic system to another from authoritarianism and totalitarianism to new forms of democracy.

We are also witnessing a new crisis in the Western countries. In this crisis elements of ideology, political philosophy, economic and politics are combined. There is no doubt that the methods of economic management and political democracy which have been so successful until now are showing signs of obsolescence. New contradictions are becoming more and more acute in all democratic countries. Each of those countries, and the west as a whole, must try new methods and must find new forms better applicable to every specific nation. There are no general recipes, the experience of every free market and democratic country is at the same time general and specific. Pluralism is the way of life of civilized people. As the public becomes more and more civilized the activity and development of individuals will become more diversified.

This reasoning applies to the post-colonialist countries as well. The newly-born independent post-colonial countries have but one feature in common: they liberated themselves from the oppression of the colonial power; they took their destiny into their own hands, yet they do not know how to construct their new lives. Colonialism had various forms and the colonial regimes differed from country to country. Under various colonial regimes each nation preserved its uniqueness. It is no wonder that after the liberation the new nations preferred to follow different models.

Some have consciously chosen the ways of capitalism; many were impressed by the western ideas of both free competition and the welfare state.

On the other hand, many relatively backward nations were impressed by the Communist regimes. In every post-colonial country there were politicians who believed that the communist experience guaranteed faster progress and more possibilities for overcoming cultural backwardness quickly.

The ensuing collapse of the Communist system and the crisis in the western hemisphere compel every newly established state to reconsider its own experience, methods and institutions.

Needless to say, rhetorical reasoning is an indispensable tool for accomplishing those complicated tasks. The New Rhetoric stresses that, in order to elaborate new ways of life, one must take into account all the available knowledge and experience accumulated by the former and present social structures. The rhetorical method should be used not to deny the past but to preserve past elements which can be useful in present and future calculations.

This reasoning also shows that the construction of the new human societies must be done by the people who are more critical than ever before and at the same time more tolerant in their beliefs and cooperation.

The New Rhetoric is also a method of exhorting the public to be more civilized, knowledgeable and respectful of one another's viewpoints. Narrow-minded technocrats have had their day and have failed.

Professionalism must be accompanied by humaneness.

When we stress that the New Rhetoric is a method for finding practical solutions for the new century based on previous experience and new social awareness we imply that there is a certain direction with very general goals which should be pursued. We have no recipe for paradise but we know that at every step forward every new institution and new enterprise should tend to expand individual and social freedom, promote tolerance and a reasonable realistic approach to every question. These ideals are not derived from pure speculation, they are neither a priori nor moralistic. They are based on the evaluation of the developing trends of our culture and civilization.

Every generation has fought for justice, tolerance, security and freedom thus creating material, social and psychological forces equipped to guide our purposeful endeavors.

In this way the circle closes. The New Rhetoric is a philosophy, methodology and the pursuit of new social development.

Subject Index

Library of Rhetorics

Series editor: Michael Meyer
European Centre for the Study of Argumentation, Université Libre, Brussels, Belgium

Scope: The bookseries *Library of Rhetorics* is meant as a companion series to the international journal *Argumentation.* The bookseries and the journal should reinforce each other. The bookseries would mainly focus on:
– Argumentation *stricto sensu* (the theory of reasoning)
– Literary and legal rhetoric
– Rhetoric and the humanities
– Sociology and historical aspects of rhetorical thought
– Particular problems in rhetoric and argumentation.

Publications
1. M. Maneli: *Perelman's New Rhetoric as Philosophy and Methodology for the Next Century.* 1994   ISBN 0-7923-2166-9
2. H. Parret: *The Aesthetics of Communication.* Pragmatics and Beyond. 1993
                                                                          ISBN 0-7923-2198-7
3. E.K. Moore: *The Passions of Rhetoric: Lessing's Theory of Argument and the German Enlightenment.* 1993   ISBN 0-7923-2308-4

KLUWER ACADEMIC PUBLISHERS – DORDRECHT / BOSTON / LONDON